ADVERSARY OF MEN

Translated from the Hungarian
by LAWRENCE WOLFE

ADVERSARY OF MEN

*An Historical Fantasy
in Three Acts*

FERENC KÖRMENDI

LONDON
SECKER AND WARBURG
1941

Martin Secker & Warburg, Ltd.
22 Essex Street, London, W.C.2

First Published 1941

Made and Printed in Great Britain at
The Mayflower Press, Plymouth. William Brendon & Son, Ltd.

. . . show us the adversary of men . . .
of what fashion he is, and what is his
work, and whence he cometh forth, and
what power he hath. . . . Let us behold
him. . . .

(New Testament, Apocrypha,
Examination of Satan.)

CHARACTERS

SATAN

HITLER

DENIZENS OF HEAVEN

DENIZENS OF EARTH

DENIZENS OF HELL

ACT I

*At the rise of the curtain the stage is in complete darkness.
Off-stage, a choir is heard singing,* fortissimo :
"*Gloria in excelsis.*" . . . *The distant strains soften
as the stage is slowly illuminated and the mise en scène
is disclosed, flooded in a pale blue radiance.*

*A Conference Table stands upon a cumulus cloud
suspended in mid-air. At the head, on the right, there
is a Luminescence, merging into a dazzling Radiance.
Ranged from right to left,* BUDDHA, MOSES, THE SON,
MAHOMET, *occupy four low-backed chairs facing the
auditorium. At the foot of the table, left, stands*
SATAN. *The Archangels* MICHAEL, GABRIEL,
RAPHAEL *stand upon the cloud with their backs to the
auditorium.*

MICHAEL (*continuing his report*) : As I was saying,
O Lord, I do not know what is wrong. I have been
observing, enquiring, investigating, and yet I cannot
tell what is at fault : (*indicating the other two Archangels*)
they are as perplexed as I am.

BUDDHA : Perhaps the trouble lies in the soul,
Michael ?

MICHAEL : Partly, O Wise Buddha.

MOSES : Or has the body deteriorated ?

MICHAEL : The body is not perfectly sound, either,
O Lawgiver.

THE SON : There may be something wrong with the
emotions ?

MAHOMET : Or with the way of thought ?

MICHAEL : The emotions have become confused,
O Saviour—and thought has gone astray, O Prophet.

7

SATAN (*with explanatory gesture, to the Light*): The situation is quite clear—the whole concern is now out of gear. The different phenomena are interconnected, and the connections are obvious. Where there is famine to-day, there will be war to-morrow; and where there is war to-day, there will be famine to-morrow. This is only one example out of many. I don't wish to brag about my successes, but for a long time now there's been an increasing tendency down there to accept my policy.

MICHAEL: You are mistaken, Satan; the churches are full.

SATAN: And what are the people thinking of while they listen (*gesture towards the Four*) to your priests? According to my reliable information they're thinking chiefly of business and copulation. And their ailments.

RAPHAEL: The health situation is not at all bad. Medical science has made considerable progress during the past century or so and physically sound and strong generations have grown up everywhere.

SATAN: Quite. Indeed, sometimes and in some places there have been too many of them, so that every now and then they have been killing each other off by the million—and in between times they have been establishing new records, such as long-jump records . . . or writing pacifist poetry.

GABRIEL: The emotions have become more refined and have made human relationships more complete: thought is also serving the commonweal through science and art.

SATAN: The refinement of the emotions! You mean that sentiment has turned into sentimentality. As to thought, it is mostly compromise. (*To the Archangels animatedly.*) Your talk sounds rather confused, my

8

friends—no wonder, since you're dealing with the Earth. At first you complain of the soul, the body, the emotions, the way of thought, then you act as if everything was in order. Is it to defend yourselves ? Or is it merely to contradict me ? (*Vehemently.*) You've failed in your work ! Of course, your failure is to my benefit, but that is not the purpose of the concern ! I've always had my bit of profit and I mean to go on having it, but we must be fair—however welcome that would be to me personally, the Fundamental Articles do not stipulate that everything is to go to the bad of itself ! It's all your fault.

MAHOMET : No quarrelling, Satan.

MOSES : Quiet, Evil One !

SATAN (*to the Light, plaintively*) : He's beginning to use those old-fashioned sobriquets again !

THE SON (*gently*) : Do not quarrel, please. You started it, Satan. There is no time for strife while man is waiting for salvation. We must settle the matter with love.

BUDDHA : And wisdom.

SATAN (*waving his hand*) : Or in some other way. Where love and wisdom have misfired we must have recourse to some other method. I've been watching the situation on the Earth and I have certain ideas on the subject. (*Enthusiasm.*) What is required on Earth is a different management, a different direction, O Lord, a different order, a different system. The concern is facing bankruptcy, with errors and trouble everywhere. Yet it cannot be said that the basic idea was mistaken or that the present management is incompetent. (*Wide gesture.*) Buddha ! Moses ! The Saviour ! Mahomet ! What a Board ! And their agents : the Archangels, Saints, Prophets, Martyrs,

Sages, Thinkers, Doctors of the Church, the Possessed, the Priests, the Missionaries, the Disciples ! No incompetence there ! The work has been divided among them more or less appropriately and the material itself, Man—well, I may say without flattery and to your glory, O Lord, he is not bad, at least he is not essentially worse than the other living creatures on Jupiter or Saturn or on any of the trillion trillion other estates of Infinite Universe Incorporated, though he might be younger and different. Then what is wrong with him ? (*To the Four, professorially.*) The fact that what you have given to Man is much, but not sufficient. It is not all. It is not the *whole.* (*To* BUDDHA.) Beside your wisdom there is unwisdom. (*To* MOSES.) Beside your morality there is immorality. (*To* THE SON.) Beside your loving-kindness there is evil and (*to* MAHOMET) beside your faith there is unbelief. What is lacking down below is *completeness.* That is what is wrong : your work lacks completeness. It cannot be otherwise. (*Graceful, conceited gesture towards himself.*) There's only one thing that can be complete : evil. (*To the Light suddenly, persuasively.*) I have a grandiose scheme, O Lord— leave the Earth entirely to me for a time.

BUDDHA : What a stupid idea !

MOSES : An impertinence !

THE SON : An evil stratagem !

MAHOMET : Lying conceit !

THE VOICE : Silence, my children. Let us hear his scheme. (*To* SATAN.) You want the Earth ? And what do you propose to do with it ?

SATAN : Thank you, O Lord, for your interest (*very deliberately*), but do not ask for details now. You know, O Lord, that what I undertake I perform efficiently. If I have not scored any decisive success on the Earth so far it is not my fault. They (*pointing at the Four*) have prevented me from working according to my bent and capacity. The competition I have had to contend with has been colossal and my own means limited. I have been unable to raise any temples, and even the little propaganda I have been able to make had to be made in secret. . . . But if I am given a free hand for a time and you (*to the Four, reproachfully*) refrain from interfering, I will carry out the Great Test and bring about a Decision. I will put the concern in order by creating a clear-cut issue. . . .

THE VOICE: But how? What do you propose to do? Answer me.

SATAN: It is very simple, O Lord. Everything I do will be the exact contrary of what they (*indicating the Four*) approve and would do themselves. But I will act completely, comprehensively, without any gaps. (*Modestly, but naturally.*) I will do evil.

BUDDHA: I do not see any sense in this scheme.

MOSES: What result can it produce other than evil!

THE SON: A vile plot.

MAHOMET: It's shamelessly selfish, without a trace of a good intention.

SATAN (*protesting*): Really! Even the way to my realm is paved with good intentions. In any case, if Man does not like what I offer him he will recoil from it and return to you. And if he finds that I suit him, then . . . well, then to hell with him!

THE VOICE: I see, Satan. You want to try a bold experiment and you want a high price for it. I will consider it.

SATAN: Very well, O Lord. But . . . remember that whereas your great work, as a whole, is infinite both in time and space, the Earth with its few hundred

million square mile: and in less than ten thousand years
has given you much care and vexation, all on account
of Man. Of course, I myself had some little share in
this, but that is embodied in the Articles. Remember,
O Lord, that whereas your Univer es and Worlds are
so numerous that even I do not know their number,
there is none among them that is less worthy of your
Spirit than the Earth. (*Persuasively*.) What is wrong
with the Sun ? It glows, illuminates the heavens,
belches fire ; its creatures are faithful to your laws.
What is wrong on Venus and Mars ? What is wrong
on the Vega and in the Milky Way ? Nothing. Everything speeds along, spins or revolves in obedience to
your will. That which is transient passes and that
which you commanded to survive survives. But the
Earth, O Lord ! It has given you pain and disillusion-
ment, and disappointment upon disappointment has
been the share of the management. Good hardly begins
to sprout before it is infested with Evil—for as I have
said, I am greatly in favour down there. Well, let them
have what they want.

THE VOICE: There is only one Will, Satan, do not forget.

BUDDHA
MOSES
THE SON
MAHOMET
$\left.\right\}$ (*simultaneously*) : Amen.

SATAN : Forgive me, O Lord. It is so. The Will
belongs to you. (*Over-zealous*.) Everything belongs to
you, O Lord, I know. But the inhabitants of the
Earth keep forgetting this, or evading it whenever
they can. Have you the time to occupy yourself so
much with the Earth and Man ? To bother with them.

THE VOICE (*somewhat taken aback*) : Bother ? You
say bother ?

SATAN (*quickly, incisively*) : Yes, O Lord, yes. You bother with them a great deal, bother with them continually. (*Sweeping gesture.*) On the Cassiopeia you rearranged the seas by a single touch—on the Earth they have been vexing you for five thousand years (*with an edge towards* MOSES) by persecuting your Chosen People.

MOSES (*irritably*) : Your irony is wasted, Satan. My people, hardened in suffering, remains the Chosen People.

SATAN : I do not know whether I should congratulate Israel on this fact or the Lord. (*To the Light.*) You created the Pleiades with a wink, and down on the Earth there was conflict as to the extent of the Empire of the Cæsars. While, with a nod, you established a new order for Force and Matter on Orion, Man on Earth was maltreating your only begotten Son.

THE SON (*modestly*) : Let us forget about it, Satan.

SATAN : I know. You've forgiven them. But I do not forget so easily. (*To the Light.*) A breath from your nostrils was sufficient to settle the immutable laws of the distribution of air in space—on the Earth they all called upon you while butchering each other for the possession of mountains and rivers. On Phœnix you determined with a single· thought the ultimate values of the elements ; on the Earth the peoples fought, so that other peoples should have less to eat. In moments of a thousand million years you fashioned reason, gave meaning to order, brought order into universes, balancing matter and spirit ; upon Earth confusion grew worse confounded and spawned vexation. Your laws were only used to be broken, your spirit to be mocked, and the Earth itself became the hotbed of a virulent disease—hate—that may infect the Universe.

MOSES (*angry*): That is a libel! (*Indicating his group.*) Apart from ourselves, how many men have served the Lord so gloriously that what they have created will live so long as there is an Earth and there are men upon it!

SATAN: I know, O Lawgiver, I know. I suppose you now want to enumerate Confucius, King David, Aristotle, Pythagoras, Plato, Phidias, St. Paul, St. Francis of Assisi, Dante, Michelangelo, Shakespeare, Goethe, Kant, Beethoven, Dostoevsky, Einstein, Freud and all the rest. . . . All right. I know about them. I possess a universal education, I even own an encyclopedia. (*Imitating* MOSES'S *tone.*) Quite apart from the Four of you, their individual merits are certainly indisputable. But what is the outcome of it all? To mention only the most recent times—I say, Michael, how many copies of Tolstoy's *War and Peace* were sold last year? In all languages, all over the Earth?

MICHAEL (*somewhat embarrassed*): Three thousand and seventy-two.

SATAN: What were the losses in the world war?

MICHAEL (*perturbed*): Eleven million dead, twenty million wounded and disabled, seven million prisoners of war, nine million civilian dead due to epidemics and general privation. Forty-three per cent of the goods produced was destroyed, as well as fourteen per cent of the means of production. The general standard of life——

SATAN: Thanks. Now, the Great War is over. I say, Gabriel, what about peace?

GABRIEL: The deliberations of the Peace Conference are proceeding. At the moment the problem is whether in the case of certain territories the *de jure* situation should adapt itself to the *de facto* situation or the other

way round. For example, they want to mutilate
Hungary, and——

SATAN : Thanks, Gabriel. Raphael, has anything
important happened since the Armistice ?

RAPHAEL : Anything important ? Apart from the
Russo-Polish conflict, or the troubles in the Baltic, or
the Japanese machinations in the Far East, or the
famine on the Volga——

SATAN : That'll do, Raphael. (*To the Light.*) Wilt
thou grant my request, O Lord ?

THE VOICE : I want to know what you propose
to do.

SATAN : All I am clear about at the moment is the
principle. As regards the details, with thy leave, O Lord,
I will extemporise. The result I guarantee. One thing
is certain : I will lead Man to the parting of the ways ;
I will tolerate no hesitancy, no vague situations. Man
must either return definitely to thee or he will have
proved that he is unworthy of thy further attention—
and in that case . . . (*persuasively*) I shall have relieved
thee of a heavy and superfluous burden. I ask for the
Earth as my reward. My present premises are somewhat inadequate as it is. Of course, I have not overmuch to do in the Universe, but my breed is increasing
and Hell was made rather narrow originally.

THE SON : Are you going to talk about property
and its allocation again ?

THE VOICE : Let him be, my Son. (*To* SATAN.)
There is sense in what you are saying, Satan. But
before I give you leave to experiment I want to know
what methods you propose to employ. I do not want
to inflict unnecessary suffering on Man.

SATAN : Suffering is never unnecessary, O Lord. The
sinner it purifies, the innocent it exalts. In any case,

the majority of sufferers are themselves responsible, while as to the minority, who suffer without deserving it . . . (*gesture*) well, it is so stipulated in the Articles. (*Objectively.*)   My method is this : I will create a great man, breathe my personality into him, then leave the rest to him.

MOSES : Great men always make trouble.

SATAN : That's just it.   That's what we want—that there should be trouble.   If there weren't any trouble (*bowing his head in the direction of the Light*) Thy Kingdom would long have come upon Earth.   Let there be trouble.   That will be the great test.   I will clarify matters, intelligently, honestly.   So then : I will create a great man.

THE VOICE : Who will it be ?   What will he be like ?

SATAN : It is too early to say, O Lord.   In any case, I will see to it that he should do his work completely. As to who it will be—in the hope of thy retrospective consent I have already done a little work in the matter ; I have already made my choice.   My attention was drawn to him by accident, when he was still a little boy.   With thy leave, I will present him.   (*He turns away, extending his right arm.*)   Braunau, in Austria, a few years before the turn of the century.

> *Part of the darkened left-hand half of the stage becomes illuminated.   We see the corner of a room, two whitewashed walls with a brown door in one, a low window in the other.   A* BOY *is standing by the window. A* WOMAN *in the doorway, having just entered.*
>
> *All eyes from the Conference Table are turned in this direction.*

THE WOMAN (*reproachfully*) : Adolf, Adolf . . . how

often have I told you that you mustn't be cruel to animals. It's inhuman to hurt even a fly. What have you done again?

THE BOY: Nothing, mother.

THE WOMAN: My dear child, I keep begging you not to tell lies and you still go on. An honest boy must confess if he's done wrong. I saw from the yard what you were doing. You were catching flies from the window-pane and tearing off their wings and legs. Aren't you sorry for them? They're God's creatures, too.

THE BOY (*shrugs defiantly and turns away*).

SATAN (*towards the Conference Table, in an undertone*): You see? He is cruel and untruthful.

THE WOMAN: Adolf, promise me you won't do it again and won't lie.

THE BOY: Oh, leave me alone.

THE WOMAN: How dare you talk to me like that! Don't you know your Ten Commandments? " Honour thy father and mother," it says——

THE BOY (*interrupting*): It's all bunk. I'll live long without that.

SATAN (*towards Conference Table*): Coarse, overbearing, conceited. (*To* MOSES.) Your teachings haven't done him much good.

MOSES (*angry*): Scoundrel!

THE WOMAN: For heaven's sake, Adolf, aren't you afraid of God? (*Crosses herself and him.*)

THE BOY: I'm not afraid of God. There isn't one, anyhow.

THE WOMAN: O Lord, help me! You're heading for damnation, Adolf! (*Sudden step towards him.*) Is this my child? I won't have you say such terrible things!

THE BOY (*menacingly*): Don't you hit me, mother, or you'll get it back!

THE WOMAN (*beside herself*): You'd strike your own mother! (*Smacks his raised hand.*)

THE BOY (*without hesitation gives her a hard blow on the hand.*)

THE WOMAN (*gives a scream.*)

> The scene is suddenly blotted out.

SATAN (*turns towards Conference Table in the pale blue radiance*): He struck his mother. That blow will haunt him all his life. The sense of guilt will continually rise to torment him and drive him to haunt his parents' graves. Not a bad thing—I'll exploit it. (*Pause, then gesture.*) Here's something else. Linz, Austria again, several years later.

> *Left-hand half, upstage, lights up. Rows of school desks. At the end of the first desk sits an* ADOLES-CENT. *The* TEACHER *is standing in front of the desks.*

THE TEACHER: What date was Rudolf of Habsburg born? Well, Adolf? (*Points to him.*)

THE ADOLESCENT (*rises clumsily*): Rudolf of Habsburg was born . . . (*Breaks off with stupid grimace.*)

THE TEACHER: Well, son?

THE ADOLESCENT (*is silent, shrugs his shoulder, gazes at the floor*).

THE TEACHER: Speak out, Adolf. Or don't you know?

THE ADOLESCENT (*looks at him, then back at the floor, shrugs*).

THE TEACHER: I see. Then you haven't done your homework?

THE ADOLESCENT (*after a silence, indifferently*): No.

SATAN (*towards Conference Table*) : This sounds like frankness, but it's only impertinence. He's a lazy, negligent youth .

BUDDHA (*angry*) : Stupid fellow !

THE TEACHER : But even if you haven't done your homework you ought to know this. I talked about it only yesterday. (*Brief pause, then, suspiciously.*) Tell me, Adolf, who was Rudolf of Habsburg ?

THE ADOLESCENT : Rudolf of Habsburg—— (*Breaks off, shrugs.*)

THE TEACHER (*angry*) : Didn't you listen when I was talking about him ? So you just sit there and stare without listening to the lessons ? What ?

SATAN (*towards Conference Table*) : Inattentive, uncultured.

THE ADOLESCENT (*indifferently*) : No, I didn't listen.

THE TEACHER : Impertinent brat ! Get into the corner !

THE ADOLESCENT (*challenging look, impudently*) : I won't !

THE TEACHER (*beside himself*) : Get into the corner or——

THE ADOLESCENT (*interrupting*) : You're not going to put me to shame. (*Leaves classroom with defiant bearing, slamming the door behind him.*)

    The scene is blotted out.

SATAN (*towards Conference Table*) : Vain, violent, disrespectful. (*Gesture towards left.*) Here's something else. Vienna, the first decade of the new century.

    Lights. Part of an office. A Biedermeyer desk, behind it an easel. The PROFESSOR *is standing by the desk, facing him is a* YOUNG MAN. *A heap of paintings, drawings, sketches on the desk.*

THE PROFESSOR : Sorry, my young friend. I've carefully examined all this. I must be frank—they're feeble, childish experiments. That in itself wouldn't matter. It is the task of the Academy to discover new talent and develop it. But that is just it—talent. I cannot detect any talent here. (*Picks up picture.*) The choice of theme, the draughtsmanship, the brushwork, the perspective, the colours, the conception—it all reveals a painful oil-print style. You do possess a certain dexterity. In other words, it is evident that you have decided to become an artist. But intention is not enough. I cannot let you join the Academy.

THE YOUNG MAN : Please, Herr Professor, don't drive me to despair. Perhaps you're mistaken ? Perhaps you haven't examined them carefully enough ? I know they're good. I know I've talent. I know I'm going to be a great artist. Please have another look—— (*Snatches up a picture.*)

THE PROFESSOR : My dear young friend——

THE YOUNG MAN (*interrupting*) : If you took me in hand, you with your great art could bring out what there is in me. You'll be proud of me one day, Herr Professor. (*Shaking the picture in his hand.*) Look at this : " Birth of Rudolf of Habsburg." What a theme ! Of course, this is only a sketch, but I'm going to do it one day, I'm going to do it as a fresco on a huge wall, the wall of a church, no, the wall of the throne room in the Hofburg ! Gigantic figures, gigantic lines, and what colours. . . . (*Makes movements like a house-painter.*)

THE PROFESSOR : I say, young man. . . . The art of painting is something different from . . . house-painting.

THE YOUNG MAN : Please, Herr Professor, don't

laugh at me. Don't ruin me. Don't destroy my
dreams. I must become an artist! Don't you realise
that . . . that . . . (*searching for an argument*) that it's
your duty to accept me into the Academy? You
cannot exclude me . . . just because . . . (*sudden rage*)
because you don't like my face or because I paint in a
different way. (*His voice rises, changes to a hoarse screech.*)
You must help me! I need understanding! I do not
paint what the fashionable stencil artists or the ossified
old idiots paint! I paint with my heart and soul, I
paint with my blood! I believe in what I paint!
(*Bellowing.*) My colours are the colours of a new world.
My lines are the lines of a new art.

THE PROFESSOR (*staggered*): Please don't bellow.
(*Suddenly angry, snatches up a picture from desk.*) Where's
the new art in this? You talk about stencil artists and
old idiots! Why, this is banal, full of clichés—it's
worse, it's done under a mixture of influences, indeed,
it's nothing but an imitation! It wouldn't be so bad
if you hadn't chosen the worst painters to imitate, if
you hadn't copied the most commonplace features, but
that's what you have done. (*Gathers up pictures.*) Here
—please go away. (*A little more courteously.*) I'm
sorry.

THE YOUNG MAN (*bawling*): Don't send me away!
I demand that you accept me! I'm going to show
you people——

THE PROFESSOR: How dare you talk in that tone!
You can't terrorise me. What are you waiting for?
Shall I have you put out by the commissionaire?
Good morning!

THE YOUNG MAN (*baiting*): You're old and envious
and untalented, you people, so you try to suppress us,
the young and talented. Well, I'll show you! You're

in the pay of the Jews! (*Slowly retreats, staring fixedly at the* PROFESSOR.)

> *Scene fades out.*

SATAN (*towards Conference Table*): Untalented, but consumed with ambition. A heavy blow to his artistic dreams. He's suspicious and vengeful. (*Gesture towards left.*) Here's something else. Vienna again, a few years later.

> *Scene lights up. Front wall of house in course of completion. Pair of steps against front door, on them stands a* HOUSE-PAINTER. *He is painting top of the door with characteristic up-and-down movements and whistling the waltz from the " Merry Widow." Cowbell signals dinner interval. The* HOUSE-PAINTER *deposits paint pot and brush and sits on top of steps.*

THE HOUSE-PAINTER: Time to eat. Bread and sausage. Can't afford anything else. Forty-eight heller per hour. Twelve hours' work a day—if there is any work. What's the use? The architect makes money, the contractor makes money, the builder makes money, the owner makes money, the palace is ready for the tenants, they all make money. All Jews. And I? I can starve to death on forty-eight heller an hour. Why? Because capital is exploiting labour. The worker is defenceless. (*While he is talking the other workers gradually gather round.*) And why is the worker defenceless? Because the Socialists are fools and knaves. The Social Democratic Party has betrayed the workers. And why? Because the Party is in the hands of the Jews and the Jewish Executive is serving Jewish capital, not defending the Christian worker. And why? Because the Socialist leaders are getting mazumah from the Jews. (*Fidgets on the steps.*) But, of course, they also pocket the workers' dimes—membership, party tax, contributions and the devil knows what. That's why I'm not a member of the Social Democratic Party.

AN OLD WORKMAN: That's quite clear, that is. If you were a member you wouldn't be talking such rot.

THE HOUSE-PAINTER (*makes sweeping gesture with arm*): Huh, the old fellow. He's got one foot in the grave, yet he talks, though he doesn't know what he's talking about. I suppose you wouldn't like to be a little better off, eh?

A YOUNG WORKMAN: He will be, one day, and so shall we all. Our time'll come. Workers of the World, Unite!

THE HOUSE-PAINTER: Fools of the world! Idiotic theorists! You think your great Marx is going to save you. Why, he was a Jew! What are the Communist leaders doing in Switzerland? They're sitting in the coffee houses, guzzling, pocketing the Jewish money they get to keep mum! But as to you German Christian workers—just try to organise a little strike and see what happens. Or make a little demonstration —the police'll come at once and scatter you like chaff. And the boss'll kick you out. There's the flotsam and jetsam, the blacklegs, they'll work at a lower wage. And why? Because they get money from the Jews in secret. And you, you can starve until you drop or give in. And why? Because Capital is Jewish and you are Christians! (*There is now quite a crowd round him.*)

THE FOREMAN (*comes from right*): What's going on here?

THE HOUSE-PAINTER: What's that to you? It's dinner-time.

23

THE FOREMAN : If it's dinner-time then eat and rest. You can't have a public meeting.

THE HOUSE-PAINTER : None of your business ! You nigger driver ! Do you think you can order us about in our free time for that miserable forty-eight heller ?

THE FOREMAN : Shut up, or you'll get into trouble. See ?

THE YOUNG WORKMAN : Let the jack-in-the-box go on with his stunt. (*General laughter*.) It's amusing.

THE HOUSE-PAINTER : I'm a jack-in-the-box, am I ? Well, you're a poor blind animal. You can't even see what's happening to yourself. And why ? Because the Party's muddling you up with all sorts of books and highbrow education, instead of letting you realise your lot. Both capital and the workers' organisations are in the hands of the Jews ! (*Pointing at the* FOREMAN.) He's in the pay of the Jews, too.

THE FOREMAN : That'll do. Come off those steps !

THE HOUSE-PAINTER : You're slaves of the Jews, all of you ! My poor exploited German Christian fellow workers ! Until you wake up——

THE FOREMAN (*seizes steps, gives them a shake, seizes* HOUSE-PAINTER *by the leg*): Come on down. (*He gives a tug, the steps wobble, the* HOUSE-PAINTER *makes desperate efforts to balance himself ; general laughter ;* HOUSE-PAINTER *clumsily climbs down.*) Come along, my man. Whether you're organised or not, if you work here you got to work, not preach. We don't want any lazy agitators here. (*Takes* HOUSE-PAINTER *by the arm.*) Come to the office.

THE HOUSE-PAINTER : What do you want of me, you—— (*Thinking better of it, humbly.*) What is it, Mr. Foreman ?

THE FOREMAN : I've been watching you for some

time, you with your big talk. You've been sacked from a dozen jobs for inciting the workers—and for your rotten work. You're well known by now. I've kept you on because I was sorry for you, but now I've had enough. You take your wages and go. (*Goes, pushing the* HOUSE-PAINTER *in front of him.*)

THE HOUSE-PAINTER (*turning round*): Fellow-workers . . . (*Sudden rage.*) You bastards, to let him do this——

Workers disperse. Scene fades out.

SATAN (*towards Conference Table*): As you see, he has stuck to the brush. At the same time, he's more obstreperous than ever. He's a garrulous, quarrelsome, irresponsible agitator. (*Gesture towards left.*) Here's some more. And again Vienna, two or three years before the World War.

Scene lights up. Part of a dosshouse in Vienna. Window, beneath it three iron bedsteads with straw sacks. Three men are sitting on the beds ; one of them is the OUT-OF-WORK ; *he is wearing a black " cutaway."*

THE OUT-OF-WORK : . . . and so they kept chasing me on and on. I'm not wanted anywhere. (*Flings envelope onto bed.*) I've got to paint postcards—the Burg, the Stefansturm and the Town Hall. How I hate them, how I hate the whole city, the whole country. My native land ! To hell with it if it doesn't change. (*With some self-satisfaction.*) At the same time, the postcards aren't bad at all. They sell. Ten heller each. (*Sudden rage.*) That's the fate of an artist ! And why ? Because art is in the hands of the Jews ! It's they who dictate what's wanted, they want muck, naked whores, upside-down scenery—that's what they

25

call art. Unless you're a Jew or a servant of the Jews you can perish. That's why they didn't want my art. (*Darkly.*) That was why they wouldn't have me at the Academy. (*Snort.*) And what about my work, my honest toil? They didn't want that, either. They kicked me out everywhere. And why? Because I refused to hold my tongue. And I won't. I'm going to talk! Everything belongs to the Jews. The people live in misery, the workers are exploited, the peasants are dying of starvation. And it'll be like that until we disarm the Jews, take away their money, their power, every——

A VOICE·(*from the back*): Shut up! I want to sleep.

THE MAN ON SECOND BED: Hush. You're disturbing them. (*Takes off shoes, puts legs of bed into them.*) They'll kick you out of here as well if you're not careful. (*Undressing.*) You ought to be glad you got a place to sleep.

THE MAN ON THIRD BED: You're wrong, anyhow. Now, I'm a Jew. Where's my wealth, my power? How do I exploit the workers and peasants? I'm a journeyman tailor, out-of-work for a year. Besides, what do you keep on against the Jews for? Who lent you a krone the other day? Me. You took it, though you knew I am a Jew.

THE OUT-OF-WORK: You're the only honest Jew in the world. That's why you're down and out. And why? Because you're honest, so your Jewish brethren have started to persecute you. And when the Jews start on a man . . . Look at me. They cut me off from my art and took away my work. I walk in the street, a man looks at me—it's a dirty Jew watching me. It's no use my going to the Labour Exchange. "It's you, is it?" they say. "Go away, we've got no work for you." That's what they say. And why? Because they've got orders from the Jews. I'm to be persecuted, driven out of the world. And why? (*Bawling.*) Because I tell the truth! The Jews are the canker of the world!

A VOICE (*from the back*): Shut up, you! I want to go to sleep.

THE OUT-OF-WORK (*sudden whisper*): Do you hear that? The Jews won't let me speak. I can't open my mouth even here, they're after me. . . . Well, one day——

The scene fades out.

SATAN (*towards Conference Table*): A case well known to psychiatry. Maniac depressive condition. A mixture of megalomania and persecution mania. Vacillating character and temperament. There's a single obsession in the focus of the mental functions: the Jews; a single emotion in the focus of temperament: hate. (*Brief pause, then he raises his hand.*) Having reached this stage in my observations of him, I knew that he was my man. Soon after the time came for personal contact. (*Gesture towards left.*) Here! The Western Front, nineteen-seventeen, a field hospital.

Scene lights up. Part of a ward in a hospital behind the Front. Bed at right angles with auditorium, so that patient is invisible, and so are the contents of the chart above his head.

At the head of the bed, on the right, DR. SCHMIDT, a regimental surgeon; on the left, DR. KOHN, another regimental surgeon. Later, a NURSE and the VISITOR.

DR. SCHMIDT (*to PATIENT, with rough, soldierly benevolence*): Well, then, Corporal, try to sit up. One-two-three!

THE PATIENT (*makes no move ; moaning*) : I can't. I can't move. Oh, oh ! I'm blind !

DR. KOHN : Let him be, Dr. Schmidt. If he feels better lying down, let him lie. He'll sit up when he gets tired of lying on his back.

THE PATIENT : What do you mean when I get tired ? I'd sit up—if I could.

DR. SCHMIDT : A bad case, Dr. Kohn. Mustard gas. The optic nerves destroyed. The man's been blinded. Those damned British ! They use mustard gas !

DR. KOHN (*drily*) : So do we. Anyhow, I repeat I cannot agree with you. This man is not blind.

THE PATIENT (*bellicose*) : But I am. Who says I'm not blind ? Why, I can't see. (*Plaintively.*) I can't see.

DR. SCHMIDT : The optic nerves——

DR. KOHN : —are quite sound. I examined them twice.

DR. SCHMIDT : The pupils——

DR. KOHN : —react normally.

DR. SCHMIDT : Yet the patient cannot see. All your examinations are of no avail in face of the facts. The fact is that this man cannot see.

THE PATIENT (*moaning*) : I can't see.

DR. KOHN : Of course he can't. But not for organic reasons. It's *inwardly* that he's blind.

DR. SCHMIDT : What do you mean by that ? (*Distrustful.*) You know, Dr. Kohn, I don't agree with the . . . shall I say, un-German medical tendency to neglect the facts and proceed upon vague assumptions.

DR. KOHN : I know you don't agree with this tendency. But that does not alter my view. This man is only inwardly blind. There was something he did not want to see, or does not want to see, therefore he is blind. Temporarily. It is a so-called hysterical blindness. The trouble is in the mind, not in the organ. It'll pass.

THE PATIENT (*angrily shouting*) : What are you talking about, whoever you are ? What's this about hysteria ? What am I—an old Jewess ! This is Jewish talk. I was blinded by mustard gas. Gott strafe England !

DR. SCHMIDT : Don't excite yourself, Corporal. And don't be offensive to (*with a little emphasis*) Regimental Surgeon Dr. Kohn.

DR. KOHN : Don't worry about that, Dr. Schmidt. Let him shout if it's a relief to him. (*Matter-of-fact tone.*) So, in this case I am against an operation. The complaint will cease the moment the patient realises that he no longer needs it, that it's superfluous or even harmful. Perhaps a traumatic experience——

DR. SCHMIDT : But look here, you don't mean to say that the patient is malingering !

DR. KOHN : Certainly not. He's not malingering. Or to be more precise : he's not consciously malingering. Hysterical blindness, as we know—— (*Breaks off as the door opens.*)

THE NURSE (*enters, stops facing the doctors*): Excuse me, there's a man outside who came to see the Corporal, he says he must see him urgently.

DR. SCHMIDT : No, Sister—it's not visiting time, and besides, as you know yourself, this patient can't have any visitors.

THE NURSE : I know, sir, but I'm reporting it because the man says he must see the Corporal on a matter of vital importance, and I thought——

DR. SCHMIDT (*breaks in*): Sorry. Tell him it's impossible.

DR. KOHN : Look here, Dr. Schmidt, it can't hurt the patient to receive a visit, can it ? The man may have travelled a considerable distance, and who knows how difficult it's been for him to get into the base hospital. A little change can only do the patient good. Give the word, Dr. Schmidt.

DR. SCHMIDT : I don't agree with you, but if you think the man ought to be admitted, well then . . . on your own responsibility. (*To* NURSE.) Show him in. (*To* PATIENT.) Well, Corporal, you're going to have a visitor.

THE PATIENT (*morosely*) : What visitor ? To hell with him !

At this moment enter, behind the NURSE

THE VISITOR (*he is visibly embarrassed, bows low to the doctors, who nod in return, then, with the* NURSE, *leave the ward ; he stands still for a moment, then comes forward, sits on chair by the bed, facing the* PATIENT) : Good morning !

THE PATIENT (*belligerently*) : Who's that ?

THE VISITOR : It's me.

THE PATIENT : " It's me, it's me ! " Who the devil's me ?

THE VISITOR : Can't you see, Corporal ?

THE PATIENT : How could I ? Can't you see I'm blind ?

THE VISITOR : Of course—I beg your pardon. (*Suddenly changes tone ; low but penetrating.*) You're blind, I know, or rather, you can't see. And what else is the matter with you ? Does the hand hurt with which you once struck your mother ?

THE PATIENT (*gives a start*) : What ? My hand . . . my mother . . .

The VISITOR : Or does your mouth hurt because you lied with it and denied that there was a God ? . . .

THE PATIENT : What are you saying ? My mouth . . . lies . . . atheism . . .

THE VISITOR: Or does your brain hurt with empti-
ness because you didn't learn anything? Or your
cheeks, because you were impertinent with your
teacher and didn't even blush?

THE PATIENT: My brain . . . my cheeks. . . .
What are you talking about? Who are you?

THE VISITOR: Or perhaps your stomach's turning
with rage because they wouldn't have you at the Academy? Or is it your own pictures that give you nausea?

THE PATIENT (*tossing in his bed*): What's this?
Who're you? What do you want of me?

THE VISITOR: Do the soles of your feet hurt from
the rungs of the steps—that time, when you were a
housepainter? Does your tongue hurt from the words
with which you tried to incite your fellow-workers?
Does your back hurt from the strawsack in the dosshouse—perhaps because you didn't deserve even that?
You're sick in body and your mind's sick from frus-
trated ambition, from gnawing envy, from burning
discontent, from consuming hatred?

THE PATIENT (*jerks himself to a sitting position; he
already wears his hair and moustache in the characteristic way
of subsequent years; his white hospital bed-jacket is decorated
with the Iron Cross; he stares at the* VISITOR *with distended
eyes*): Who are you? I don't know you. I have never
seen you. How do you know——

THE VISITOR (*waving him to silence*): Be quiet and
don't get excited—though people usually receive my
visits with some emotion. You want to know who I
am? I might say, Somebody. I might say, a Stranger.
I might say, a distant and somewhat suspicious relation. But why make a mystery of it? You'd soon find
out, anyhow. (*With a nod, as though introducing himself.*)
I'm the Devil.

THE PATIENT (*gives a violent start and emits an inarticulate cry of terror*).

THE VISITOR (*motions him to silence*): Hush! Don't make a noise. We don't want to cause trouble to the good Jewish doctor, the fool who let me in.

THE PATIENT: What do you want? . . . What did you come for? . . . I didn't ask for you.

THE VISITOR: It's enough that you've been expecting me, even if unconsciously. (*Conversationally.*) You see, you don't have to summon me deliberately at midnight with all sorts of old-fashioned hocus-pocus. An act, a flash of thought, a quiver of emotion—that's enough; if it takes my fancy I come. (*Natural tone.*) As I say, I'm the Devil and so you needn't be surprised that I know all about you, for I'm almost all-knowing. But I've kept an eye on you, especially since you struck your mother.

THE PATIENT (*groans*).

THE VISITOR: We don't want any emotional outbursts, not for the present; and certainly not in my presence. You see, frankness is an essential factor in this conversation—the opposite would be useless. (*Matter-of-factly, interrogating.*) I notice that you can see now. You can, can't you?

THE PATIENT: I can see you.

THE VISITOR: Tell me about your blindness.

THE PATIENT: It was in an attack. . . . The British. . . . Mustard gas, it was . . .

THE VISITOR (*raises hand*): Really, Adolf. . . .

THE PATIENT (*changed tone, fascinated*): I was never in the front line at all. I took no part in any attack. I didn't fight. I wasn't gassed. I don't know what happened to me. I heard the gunfire from the distance —it was awful. I got diarrhœa, collapsed. . . . I didn't want to hear or see anything. . . . When I recovered I couldn't see.

THE VISITOR: That's more like the truth. What about that? (*Pokes finger at Iron Cross.*) How did you come by it?

THE PATIENT (*in his former tone*): My bravery——

THE VISITOR (*with raised hand*): Adolf!

THE PATIENT (*again fascinated*): Once, when we were picking up the dead . . . I took it off the tunic of one of them. . . . No one saw me, so I put it in my pocket. . . . On the way to hospital, in the ambulance, I pinned it on.

THE VISITOR: That's different. Now, what next? You get better, you return to the front . . . this time right into the firing line. . . .

THE PATIENT: No! No! I won't! I can't! Why do you torment me? Mercy. . . . What do you want with me?

THE VISITOR (*simply, with satisfaction*): Well, so we've come to the point. What does the Devil usually want of a man? His soul. But I don't want yours. It's an inferior article and in any case I am not interested in petty deals. There's a great deal more at stake. (*Sweeping gesture.*) Everything! I need a suitable partner to carry the business through. Partner? No, not that—only an instrument. Say, Adolf, I took a fancy to you long ago. Your screeching voice. Your ferocious expression. Your insane stare. The through and through badness of you and your petty beastliness. The rottenness of your character, the evil of your impulses. Yes, I like you.

THE PATIENT (*fascinated*): I don't understand what you want with me.

THE VISITOR: It doesn't matter if you don't, at

first. Indeed, it's important that you should be appropriately simple-minded. (*Sudden sweeping gesture, penetratingly.*) I'm going to make you master of the world!

THE PATIENT (*strange voice*) : I thought of that myself.
. . . (*Sudden uncertainty.*) But, sir, the world's a very
big place, the task is too heavy. . . . I don't know . . .
I wouldn't dare . . .

THE VISITOR : I like you more and more every
minute. It suits my purpose that you should have
mad dreams and lack imagination, that you should be
foolhardy, yet a coward. In addition, I can sense the
cunning behind your words. You're already trying
to haggle. You hesitate, so that you might make
greater demands. Fine! But no matter how much you
ask I'll give you more. (*Penetratingly.*) You're going
to be master of men and things. Your will is to be law
upon Earth. You will be greater than the Pharaohs,
Nero, Attila, Jenghis Khan, Napoleon and the Kaiser
put together. Your strength will be greater than that
of floods and earthquakes, your power will be greater
than that of money and all the passions, you will be
mightier than the instinct of self-preservation and the
fear of death. You will saturate the Earth as pestilence
saturates its victims. You will accomplish a more
complete work than an irresistible prairie fire. Men
will worship you more than God and fear you more
than the . . . than me. Men's every passion will
belong to you : it's you they will love and hate, because
that's part of the completeness ; it's you they will
admire, you they will envy, and, above all, you they
will serve. You will be the first real Master upon Earth.
The lives of men, the fate of nations will depend on
you. You will decide how much they shall eat, whom
they shall love, how they shall love, what they shall

read. But matter will also be at your service. The
very elements will obey your commands. You can
raise a storm if you like or darken the sun; if you will,
the dung will be worth gold, and the gold will become
worthless muck. Men will think, write, compose,
paint and sculpt according to your commands. Indeed,
during your rare leisure hours you'll be able to paint
yourself—I guarantee your success in this as well.
(*Emphasis.*) You may paint a fresco on the largest wall
of the Habsburg throne room. . . . And if you like,
you may paint in blood, because men will live and die
according to your will. Whatever arouses your ire—
men, thoughts, institutions—will dissolve into nothing-
ness. Men's heart, brain, blood, muscle and the secret
force of things will all be yours. I'll make you into
something the like of which has never been upon
Earth, has never been conjured up even by the imagination. I'll give you superhuman power—you'll be but
little less even than I. And in return for all this——

THE PATIENT (*his imagination aflame, greedy, consenting*) :
What've I got to do ?

THE VISITOR (*simply*) : Evil. It seems a simple task,
yet it's difficult. I won't have any amateur performance,
or deficiencies, or compromises. You must be perfect
in evil.

THE PATIENT : I see. I would take it on, too. But
. . . doing evil and nothing but evil is an unpopular
thing and also not without danger.

THE VISITOR : That's true. But you needn't be
such a coward as all that. Firstly, I shall be protecting
you. For instance, there'll be an attempt on your life,
but it'll have been arranged by yourself, and nothing'll
happen to you. You'll be able to refer to Providence,
your avocation—that'll paralyse the power of your

enemies and will veer the sympathy of the waverers towards you, also earning you the pity of the foolish. Preach your superhuman quality and believe in it yourself. Do evil and call it good, and convince the people that it is good. Often, however, you must do evil openly. In such cases say it's true you'd done evil, but that it only hurts the minority and is to the benefit of the majority. Be mysterious and inaccessible, but sometimes behave in such a manner that everybody should think that you're charming, natural, ascetic, that you come from the people and feel well only among the people. (*Wide gesture.*) Go out and destroy! Prepare my Empire for me. At the right moment I'll come and take the Earth over from you. Your reward will be a sure place in the Minor Eternity, let us say a job for a few million years as group leader in one of my concerns, perhaps in the Drying Chamber for Bad Consciences, or . . . something like that. You understand, don't you?

THE PATIENT (*reflects, as though dissatisfied*): I understand, of course. . . . (*Sudden enthusiasm.*) All right, I'll take the job. (*Sudden depression.*) But can I do it? Aren't you over-estimating my powers?

THE VISITOR : I don't think so. In any case, I shall radiate into you the power that will intensify the required qualities in you and supply those that you lack. Give me your hand.

THE PATIENT (*reaches out hesitantly*) : Is it going to hurt?

THE VISITOR (*seizes his hand*) : It's nothing—a tingling sensation in your fingers, that's all. Feel it?

THE PATIENT : Oh !

THE VISITOR : Now it's travelling slowly upwards. Feel it? On the left side, a sort of cool heat. . . . Now it's in your chest, on the left; I'm working on your heart.

THE PATIENT: Ouch! It feels as if a stone had suddenly got into my chest.

THE VISITOR: Yes, something of the sort. Now, suddenly, you're feeling a great void in your chest.

THE PATIENT: Oh! As if something had gone out of me and there's nothing in its place.

THE VISITOR: It's the so-called soul. Don't bother about it. Now there's a sort of pressure against the back of your head. Feel it?

THE PATIENT: Ar . . . I feel giddy . . .

THE VISITOR: That's nothing. I've been doing a little something to your brain. (*Suddenly, penetratingly.*) Now look me in the eyes and repeat in a low voice what I say. (*Incisively; the* PATIENT *repeats soundlessly.*) I will serve you, Evil One, as my Lord and Master, for my pleasure and for the advent of your Kingdom. I will serve you with every evil human quality, with foolishness, dishonour, cowardice, breach of faith, untruth, betrayal, murder, blood lust, cruelty, irony, impudence, coarseness, vengefulness, stubbornness. I will serve you with all that constitutes the seven cardinal sins, with everything that is contrary to the beauty, goodness and justice of life, with everything that God despises and that corrupts the world and man. With all that I will fight for myself and for you. I know what I have to do, I know how to do it. I shall be tireless. I shall not weaken. So help me!

THE PATIENT: . . . So help me!

THE VISITOR: That's all right, then. Our contract is made. It's not the first alliance between the Devil and Man, nor the last, but I hope it'll turn out to be one of the most significant. (*Casually.*) The transaction requires assent from higher quarters, but that's my affair. (*Reflecting.*) If I can't obtain it for my present scheme, I'll give you some other commission. I'll send you to America as a gang leader. That isn't such an important task, but it's no trifle either. It'd give you plenty of scope for your talents. In any case, in a moment or two—a few years according to your reckoning—you will receive a message to start work. (*Gesture.*) Don't ask any questions, you'll know everything of yourself, I mean through me. I will give you all the help you'll need, and if you are ever in trouble or need me personally, call for me and I will come. If I summon you you must appear at once. I give you a free hand, but I'll always watch you from the corner of my eye. So be careful, for whereas we reward disloyalty, that's not the case when it is at our expense. I'm going now. I might vanish but that would be embarrassing for you people. Ring for the Nurse.

THE PATIENT (*rings with eager gesture*).

THE NURSE (*appears*) : Did you ring ?

THE PATIENT (*strong voice*) : Please, Nurse . . . this gentleman wishes to leave.

THE VISITOR (*official tone*) : Well, I was very pleased to see you, Adolf. I wish you the worst of the worst . . . er . . . the best of the best.

THE NURSE : This way, sir, then first on the left in the corridor.

THE VISITOR : Thanks, I know. Don't trouble, Sister. (*Goes.*)

THE NURSE (*closes door behind him*) : The gentleman has a limp. Is it a war wound ?

THE PATIENT (*casually*) : No. He was born with it, if I'm not mistaken.

THE NURSE: I hope, Corporal, you enjoyed the visit. But you seem somewhat upset. Your face, your eyes . . . (*low scream*). Good gracious, your look! . . . What's happened? Oh dear, I must call the doctor. . . . (*Dashes out.*)

THE PATIENT (*slowly, clumsily, gets out of bed, stands still for a moment, then comes forward*): I don't want a doctor. I can see . . . I can see everything.

Scene is suddenly blotted out.

SATAN (*resumes position at Conference Table*): That's what happened.

THE VOICE: As befits your character, they are abominations that you have shown us.

MOSES: A lawless man.

THE SON: A poor, unfortunate, straying mortal.

BUDDHA: A terrifying example of human stupidity.

MAHOMET: A ridiculous fellow.

SATAN (*politely*): All very true. But that's precisely why he's the most suitable for what I want him. (*Bowing his head towards the Light, with force.*) Have I thy leave, O Lord?

THE VOICE (*slowly*): I ought to allow the test. But tell me, Satan, why did you choose your medium from among the German people?

SATAN (*with a shrug, yet apologetically*): That was where I found him. (*Bows; persuasively.*) Then I have thy leave, O Lord?

THE VOICE (*a hard decision*): You have.

BUDDHA
MOSES
THE SON   } (*simultaneously*): No, O Lord!
MAHOMET

THE VOICE: I agree because I believe that Man

will stand the test ; because I believe that the Devil's machinations will ultimately benefit and improve him ; and because he does need a lesson.   I agree.

BUDDHA
MOSES
THE SON   } (*simultaneously*) : Thy will be done.
MAHOMET

THE CHOIR (*off*) : Now and for evermore.   Amen.

THE VOICE : I give leave, but not for ever.   Take it that I am shutting my eyes for a moment or turning my gaze away from the Earth.

> *The scene suddenly fades out, leaving only* SATAN'S *figure standing in a beam of blue light.*

SATAN (*after an instant, advances*) : So far so good.   If we are clever the Earth's going to be mine.   (*Urgently.*) Let's get on with it.   I have got the leader, and since he's German we'll call him the Fuehrer.   We must get him some associates and helpers.   (*Shrill screech of flight as he descends into the Nether Regions.   An instant's blackout, then he reappears in a red spotlight on the left ; claps his hands impatiently.*)   Hi !   Devils !

> *Devils crowd onto the scene, swarming round* SATAN.

AN OLD DEVIL : At last you're back, Master.

A YOUNG DEVIL : Any good news from the Conference ?

ALL : Is it a new job ?   Are we going to be better off ?

SATAN : Yes, a new job.   And what a job !   I persuaded Him to agree to the experiment.   He realised that there was no sense in letting the Earth mess about any longer ; it must be either—or.   He agreed.   If we fail, He will have been right—then let Him carry on with His Earth and His Man.   In that case, I think, they'll be His for evermore, and we'll have to look for something else. But if my scheme succeeds, then Man and the Earth will belong to us. At least for a few trillion years. That's something, too. The main thing is that He has recognised to a certain extent that the terms of the Articles are unfair. (*Vehemently.*) We're entitled to live and the Earth is our Lebensraum! We only have to conquer it.

ALL (*screeching*): Hear, hear! We'll conquer it.

THE OLD DEVIL (*motions crowd to silence; deliberately*): We only have a rough idea of your scheme, Master. Have you worked out the details?

THE YOUNG SCIENTIFIC DEVIL (*eagerly, in a scholarly manner*): You know, Master, that I have recently demonstrated through the sociographical data obtained by my terrestrial Mass Observation unit that owing to certain traditions, prejudices, superstitions and fixations, and, further, owing to religion and morality, all of which may be summed up as the Principle of Good, Man distrusts us, so direct action will meet with considerable difficulties and, therefore, unless we choose to face all the risks of open terrorism and revolution, re-organisation and the New Order must be prepared in such a manner that——

SATAN: Shut up! (*Motions the crowd closer with a confidential gesture.*) It's all very simple. The idea is to infect the Earth with a single idea, to have it crushed by a single man whom I will endow with all the power, to make predominant in him, and through him, evil thinking, evil instincts, evil impulses, evil intentions, in a word: Evil. The Good will be completely eradicated. (*Conceited chuckle.*) We've got some little experience in this sort of work. (*All chuckle.*) But this time I've got an absolute Power of Attorney.

41

(*Mysterious, triumphant.*) And also a new method. My task is to establish the principle, to provide the outline, to make the decision—we need not bother about the details. Let them do everything themselves up there on Earth. We'll enjoy the profits.

ALL (*chuckling, screeching, vociferous*): Hear, hear! Splendid!

ANOTHER OLD DEVIL: The idea's worthy of you, Master.

ANOTHER YOUNG DEVIL: And you are worthy yourself!

THE YOUNG SCIENTIFIC DEVIL: This method of the division or rather separation of labour and profits is strongly reminiscent of the capitalist—(*is scared into silence and jerks his head away as* AN OLD DEVIL *makes a gesture to strike him on the mouth*).

SATAN: I've already found *the* man; I've already implanted the idea in him. (*Urgently.*) Come on! We're going to organise a General Staff for him. Get me the card index of Lost Souls, German Section.

A YOUNG DEVIL *jumps to it, vanishes, instantly returns wheeling in a huge steel cabinet.*

THE YOUNG DEVIL: Here it is, Master. The data are precise, exhaustive and up-to-the-minute.

SATAN: Let me see. First of all, he must have a sort of sub-Fuehrer or substitute, someone who's worthy of him and to some extent his rival; they must be linked by a common purpose and common crimes, but they must also be jealous of each other and at times each must feel: one of us must perish. And yet they must stick to each other . . . to our advantage and benefit. (*Reaches at random into a file, takes out a card.*) Hermann Goering. (*Repeats it, as though savouring it.*)

Hermann Goering . . . not a bad name. There's something noisy and brutal about it. (*Reading from card.*) Unnaturally obese—huge head—huge muscles—strong and tough, but sluggish and lazy. Good. Unreliable, capricious, foolhardy and conceited ; secretly a coward. Excellent ! Infinitely vain, cunning and suspicious. That's what we want. Evil instincts ; a glutton ; a primitive voluptuary ; has a bent for pyromania. Splendid ! Has been in a lunatic asylum. . . . That'll do. He's the man. (*To* DEVILS.) Make a model of him !

THREE DEVILS (*get lay figure from a dark corner and rapidly start modelling*).

SATAN : He's going to be the Deputy Leader. He'll be Field-Marshal, Master of the Hunt, Master of the Horse, Master of the Bottle, Master of every damned thing. Let him also be Honorary President of some industrial exhibition. (*Reflecting.*) In fact, we may also make him Master of Economics (*glances at card*), in any case he has a pathological love for money. He's going to steal an awful lot. Show me.

THREE DEVILS (*place the Goering effigy into the red spotlight*) : Are you satisfied, Master ?

SATAN : Not bad. A pity he can only wear one uniform at a time. But he'll change often. A hundred thousand uniforms for him ! A uniform to sleep in, a uniform for copulation, a uniform for the lavatory. A separate uniform for every hour of the day, for every stirring of his thoughts. (*Staring fixedly at effigy.*) And hang it full of decorations, decorate it like a German Christmas tree.

THREE DEVILS (*decorate effigy's chest, shoulders, belly and even sides with glittering medals, glossy braid, wide coloured ribbons*) : All right, Master ?

43

SATAN (*examines the half-size effigy contentedly*): That's right. Now then. We want someone to keep the people in a state of terror in the name of the Fuehrer and the Cause. A sort of super-policeman—something of a soldier and also something of a hangman. (*Takes out a card at random.*) Hjalmar Schacht—economist—eccentric. . . . No good for this purpose, but perhaps I'll use him for something else. Let him confuse finance and economy. (*Takes out another card.*) Heinrich Himmler. Bloodthirsty—vengeful—stupid—stubborn —violent—cunning—cruel—very good. Make a model of him!

THREE DEVILS (*work zealously on the second effigy*).

SATAN: He'll be the leader of some barbarous Storm Troop organisation. (*Reflecting.*) And head of the secret political police. He'll torture masses of people, some with his own hands. Later, he will extend his activities to other countries. He'll be the first to appear in the vanquished countries (*guffaw*) to make order, maintain discipline. . . .

THREE DEVILS (*place Himmler effigy into red spotlight*): All right, Master?

SATAN: You might've made his face more bestial. Well, no matter, it'll develop. Put him beside the other one. Now we want an expert on foreign affairs, a real trouble maker. (*Contemptuously.*) Considering the quality of European diplomacy, he won't have a hard task. (*Turns over cards.*) Robert Ley—a won't work—drunkard. . . . No, we'll put *him* where his qualities have better scope. Say, let him be the leader of the workers' organisations. (*Turning over cards.*) Rudolf Hess—embittered æsthete—reserved—spiteful —dangerous. . . . No good, either. But he'll do as a sort of Secretary. He'll help his Fuehrer to write some sort of a book on some sort of a *Weltanschauung*. They'll both satisfy their literary ambition through this. He can do other work as well—say, as a personal spy or informer. Make a model! (*Turns over.*) Joachim von Ribbentrop.

A SMALL DEVIL : What disease ?

SATAN : Idiot. That's his name. An excellent name. You hear it and you at once visualise a big German with a monocle. (*Reading from card.*) Champagne traveller—second-hand gentleman—universal orrower—embezzler — garrulous — liar — swaggerer— lust for power. Yes, he'll do. Make a prototype of the so-called new diplomat !

THREE DEVILS (*work on a lay figure, then place it into red spotlight*) : All right, Master ?

SATAN : Yes. Next. We want a sort of bloodhound, some bestial figure with the soul of a butcher. Someone who terrifies, yet nauseates, a monster who is ridiculous, a nightmarish figure. . . . (*Looking at cards.*) Julius Streicher—brutal—quarrelsome—dirty fighter—stupid—base—master of coarse incitement. . . . The very thing. We might have him start a paper, to excite the masses with some absurd slogan. . . . I'll decide later what it's to be. A model of him !

THREE DEVILS (*prepare it, place it into red spotlight*) : All right, Master ?

SATAN : Not bad. In fact, quite good. (*Takes a closer look.*) Good Hell, how disgusting. Excellent. And now (*reflecting*) what else do we want ? Of course —a master of propaganda. One who repeats some silly thing until the masses give in and are convinced that it's pure wisdom. One who has a flair for nerve-racking detail and effective mob appeal. Haven't we got some mouthwash publicity man or an impresario ?

(*Looks in file.*)   Alfred Rosenberg . . . confused brain
—monomaniac—*exalté*. . . . No good for a propaganda chief.   We'll get him to write the " mythology "
of the movement.   (*Turns over.*)   Baldur von Schirach.
. . . Pathological love for children.   Excellent.   We'll
make him leader of the youth movement.   He's no
propaganda chief, either.   (*Turns over.*)   Ernst von
Roehm.   Murderer—homosexual—sadist. . . . Interesting—the qualities almost of fuehrership.   Let him be
the open rival, the dangerous rival.   I'll see what I
can do with him.   No good for propaganda, though.
(*Turns over.*)   Frick. . . . (*Murmurs something.*)   Frank
. . . (*murmurs*)   Heydrich . . . (*murmurs*)   Lutze . . .
(*murmurs*).   Yes, they all have some fine evil qualities,
something inhuman, bestial.   (*Casually.*)   Make models
of them by all means, but for propaganda . . . (*Turns
over cards.*)   Mueller . . . Mayer . . . Schmidt . . .
Schulz . . . Sub-leaders of various degrees, but no
good for propaganda. . . . (*Other cards.*)   Horst
Wessel . . . evil—corrupt—ladykiller—bully—bloodthirsty and at the same time masochist. . . . Let him
be the martyr of the movement, the legendary hero.
. . . But as to propaganda chief . . . (*Looks over the
row of effigies thoughtfully, passes in front of them.*)   Propaganda chief ? . . . (*Impatiently flicks his fingers through
cards, slams drawer.*)   Where do I get a propaganda
chief ?   Not one of them is suitable.   (*Angrily passes
in front of effigies, suddenly stops.*)   If I can't find one
among the Germans I'll have one of you devils.
(*Sweeping gesture.*)

ALL (*retreat with a scared murmur*) : Not me. . . .

SATAN (*impatient persuasiveness*) : It must be one of
you.   I must have a propaganda chief !   (*Pointing at a
YOUNG DEVIL.*)   It might be you.   If I remember

46

aright, you possess the necessary qualities. Just imagine—you'll have to hypnotise two thousand million people into believing that the Fuehrer is the greatest man in the world. You'll beflag the cities ! (*Rousingly.*) Huge banners—trumpets—vast crowds. . . .

THE YOUNG DEVIL (*badly embarrassed, painfully pro-testing*): Master . . . if you don't mind . . . I don't . . . I really know nothing about propaganda. . . . You want a more experienced devil. And . . . forgive me, Master, I consider propaganda somewhat vulgar. . . . I have other ambitions in life. . . . I'm interested in the technique of boiling the damned in oil. . . .

SATAN (*angrily*): Boiling in oil ! Foolish fellow ! What's that as compared with boiling millions of men and women in stupidity, stewing them in lies, soften-ing them in a thousand type-vats, in a liquor of words, at the various tone-temperatures, until they become a mash, with the marrow boiled out of their bones, the heart out of their bosoms, the brain out of their skulls, and they bawl in chorus what you dictate ! You say it's vulgar ! Why, that's the very essence of the thing —that it is vulgar. If you want to do something dis-tinguished, go and make a budget speech in the British Parliament. (*Turns away from him contemptuously, looks over the other devils, points at an* OLD DEVIL.) Perhaps you'll do. Come here. You'll be the propa-ganda chief and direct the press and public opinion.

THE OLD DEVIL (*scared*): Master, not me. I'm more than seven hundred million years old, I lack elasticity and . . . (*low, shy, but dignified*) and besides, I come of a good family. . . .

SATAN (*angry*): Go away ! (*Points at another* OLD DEVIL, *persuasively*.) You look experienced. I like the look of you. Step forward, please.

THE OTHER OLD DEVIL (*stammering*): It's a great honour. . . . Thank you, Master, (*somewhat reproachful*) for having at last noticed me, now, at the age of eleven hundred million years. . . . But I don't like the racket any more, and I've also learned not to be ambitious (*reproachful emphasis*) from my more successful colleagues. I get frequent backaches. I'm afraid I wouldn't make good. You want a younger devil for this sort of thing.

SATAN (*impotent rage*): I'm not in need of advice. You're all afraid. What the man's got into you! You always complain you haven't enough to do, that I'm neglecting you. . . . You all feel you're misunderstood infernal geniuses, yet now when I want to entrust one of you with a really devilish task you whine . . . (*imitating*) I'm too young . . . I'm too old . . . I get backaches . . . I want other work . . . I'm not going to have it! (*Bellowing.*) I simply command you—(*Raises arm, but before he can point at anyone*).

A VERY OLD DEVIL: Master, do not act in haste. If you appoint an unwilling devil the work'll be spoiled. Never within infernal memory has anything evil resulted from an angry decision. I have an idea, Master. Some twenty years ago you allowed one of our younger colleagues to visit the Earth and made him see the light in Germany. Do you remember?

SATAN: Ah! You're right. We used to call him Runty, didn't we? Well, what about him?

THE VERY OLD DEVIL: He lives under the name of Joseph Goebbels up there. I feel he'd be suitable for the role in question. Down here he used to be coarse, quarrelsome, untruthful, tough, and he had a hooligan cleverness. I'm sure he can't be very particular for he's been living among men on Earth, or to be more precise, among Germans, for two decades.

SATAN : There's something in what you say.

THE VERY OLD DEVIL (*persuasively*) : Besides, as far as I know they have infected him up there with human vanity and ambition, and so far he's had scarcely any successes. He obtained a degree in Philosophy at Heidelberg. (SATAN *makes a contemptuous gesture.*) He has been writing poetry, but has been unable to sell it to the literary periodicals. He has tried his hand at political journalism as well, but his articles have never got past the waste-paper basket at the daily papers. He has also written plays, but the managers have been returning them in a hurry.

SATAN : Not bad.

THE VERY OLD DEVIL : He's full of bitterness, so much so that he sometimes forgets he's a devil and feels a persecuted human genius, with other humans jealous of his talent. Finally, as regards his character, I'm sure he'll have no difficulty in assuming all those good, I mean bad, I mean . . . well, all those human characteristics that a plain devil requires in order to become an excellent propaganda chief—that is, if he hasn't got them already.

SATAN : Summon Runty.

A LITTLE DEVIL : Yes, Master. (*Skips to a huge telephone*) : Hello Interstellar Exchange. . . . This is Hell number 1. I want the Earth, Northern Hemisphere, Europe, Germany, Berlin. . . . I want a special nerve-line, extra-rapid personal call to devil number onehundredbilliontwenty-eight. You'll find him under the name of Joseph Goebbels, Miss. (*Importantly.*) It's urgent. The Master wants him. (*After an instant.*) Hello, Runty ! Master wants you. At once. No, you must leave everything. Evil-bye. (*Hangs up, turns round.*) He's coming, Master.

Devils open an avenue for someone arriving from imaginary entrance.

RUNTY (*in mufti, somewhat out of breath, stops before* SATAN): Here I am, Master. I came at once, hadn't even time to change, only just had time to jump on the first infernal ray. Command me, Master.

SATAN: The matter's urgent. I'll be brief. I've obtained authority (*gesture*) up there to corrupt the world. The stake is the Earth. Our chances of success are good. I've made all arrangements, but we haven't got a propaganda chief. He must work up there in human shape. In his own sphere I will give him unlimited power. Indeed, he will be the secret impeller of men, things and events to a considerable extent. . . . Listen. (*Puts left hand on* RUNTY'S *shoulder, makes hypnotic movements with right.*) Do you understand?

RUNTY: I do, Master.

SATAN: Will you do it?

RUNTY (*taken aback, somewhat wryly*): Me? . . . Well, I must confess . . . yesterday I at last managed to have a private talk, at an exclusive party, you know, with the manager of the International Jewish Experimental Theatre and he promised to read my new comedy and give me an answer within a week. . . .

SATAN (*vehemently*): Stop that nonsense! Your task'll be not to write any sort of play, but to stage-manage a real drama of horror—anyhow, that'll be part of your task. You will direct the theatre, literature and art in Germany and later on all over the world. I will place in your hands music and science as well. I will subordinate to you the entire culture of the Earth.

RUNTY: Yes, Master, I understand. It's a big thing. But it so happens that I have just had an inquiry from a publisher for my volume of poems. It's true he's a member of the Socialist Party, but he's a fine man and an enthusiastic lover of literature.

SATAN (*more vehement*): You'll do the propaganda in the name of your Fuehrer and the Cause, and you'll have full power. You can raise and crush the peoples with your propaganda, just as you like. You can undermine the life of the nations with it, poison it. You shall be the sole judge of what human brains have created or will create in the future. You will rouse or strike down millions of people, fire the passions, direct human thought, control human taste, govern education. All this you will do on behalf of your Fuehrer, but you'll have even greater power than he in your sphere, and even outside it, for you will be influencing his spirit as well. (*Bellowing.*) Propaganda! (*Suddenly, in a low, penetrating tone.*) You can hang any-one who writes better poems and plays than you. You can have all who have refused to publish or produce your work tortured to death. (*Insinuatingly.*) You can make your rivals fail, for you'll have all the means in your hands, and particularly the mind of the masses.

RUNTY (*stands ruminating for a moment, then*): My rivals. . . . (*Suddenly bows low.*) Thanks, Master. I accept.

ALL (*screeching*): Hip, hip, hurrah!

SATAN (*wipes brow*): At last. So it's settled. (*Sudden start.*) But . . . umm. . . . It may upset things that . . . (*points at* RUNTY'S *foot*) won't they see your cloven hoof?

RUNTY (*unexpected animation, as though already in his new role*): I'll see to it that they should regard it as natural, that they should consider it a glorious thing, a mark of distinction. I'll make it the fashion. (*Pose.*)

Fellow-countrymen ! Up till now there's been a stupid
and evil prejudice to the effect that a sound man must
have a sound foot. But what does sound mean ? It
means tediously regular, old-fashioned ! Our revolution will not tolerate these antiquated superstitions.
With the re-birth of the spirit the body's also re-born,
re-shaped. Shall I show you how ? Look ! (*Pulls
up trousers on club-foot, shows orthopedic boot, then hobbles
a few paces.*) The rhythm of the new pace ! The new
gait, the new dynamics of walking !

ALL (*surprised murmurs*).

SATAN (*laugh*) : You're quick on the uptake. I think
you're not going to disappoint me. (*Importantly.*)
And now. . . . Of course. We want an ally, a
foreigner, so they can cite each other, at times meet
for presumptuous consultations and, above all, so that
they can fête each other. Any of you got a suggestion
to make ?

RUNTY (*bawling*) : I have. Not only a suggestion,
but a candidate ! He was a Communist bricklayer,
became a Socialist editor, then an Imperialist warmonger
and a Chauvinist agitator. He's unreliable, capricious,
vain, a swaggerer, treacherous, a turncoat—an ideal
associate. His name's Mussolini.

SATAN : I seem to remember him. A little fat man.
Not bad. (*Calling behind him.*) A model of him !

THREE DEVILS (*work rapidly, then hold effigy into red
spotlight*) : Here, Master—Benito Mussolini.

SATAN (*stares at him, laughs*) : Is this he ? Of course.
You fat little bourgeois, you pitiable bald-head. (*Jovially
poking.*) Musso, my friend, it'll be a terrific strain for
you to measure up to the other brigand. Well, don't
slobber. Your role's only going to be a secondary one.
You second-rate star. You know what you ought to

do ? Pretend to revive Roman civilisation. Become a mechanised Cæsar, a rotary Cicero. Belch wisdom, so that your followers can always say afterwards that you've predicted everything. Talk in such a way that there should be no sense in it, but it should be possible to read anything at all into it. Talk confused philosophy —I'll have your dicta written on every wall in your land. When you're facing the crowd, let there be a tall hat upon your head, or stand on a balcony, so that they cannot see how puny you are. Bring disgrace upon the Italian people, misfortune upon your nation ; if they suffer you they will deserve it. (*To the Devils.*) Put him aside. You'll get him again when he's required. And now . . . (*Excited.*) Let's begin. (*Jumps to telephone.*) Interstellar Exchange ? Earth, Northern Hemisphere, Europe, Germany, Munich, Buergerbraeu. . . . Listen. . . . There are a few civilian spies and quarrelsome military officers sitting at a table. Yes, it's the noisiest. Get me that fellow with the Charlie Chaplin moustache. Quick. Hello, Adolf. I need you. Go to the latrine, shut your eyes, I'll bring you along. (*Angry.*) It won't hurt ! Ready !

Sudden blackout ; screeching sound ; red spotlight again ; all turn towards imaginary entrance.

THE MAN WITH CHAPLIN MOUSTACHE (*in well-known raincoat, hatless, appears ; feels himself all over, confused*): This has been quick. I felt as if I'd been falling. And now, of course, I'm——

SATAN : You're in hell. (*Indicating crowd behind him.*) This is the tribe of devils. (*Gesture towards the side.*) That's your General Staff, your collaborators. (*Gesture towards man.*) This is Adolf Hitler.

53

At this moment the effigies except that of MUSSOLINI *become animated. They line up in the red glare.*

SATAN : You must start work at once. A few important formalities. . . . For instance, your emblem. In view of the nature of the movement a distorted cross would be the most suitable. (*Claps hands.*) Hi ! Draughtsmen ! Make an emblem. Something terrifying, senseless, disgusting, some monstrosity of hypnotic power.

Above the scene, in the dark background, floating in the air, a swastika appears, gradually lights up, until it glows in a blood-red hue.

SATAN (*looking up*) : Good.

HITLER : Excellent.

GENERAL STAFF (*thunderously*) : Splendid !

SATAN : And now—a slogan with which you can start off. It must be something primitive, so that everyone can understand it. It must be base, so that it should appeal to the mob instinct. It must be cruel, harmful, senseless, stupid. . . . It must be contagious like the plague, so that it should spread rapidly and infect everyone. To be on the safe side, let it be directed against a defenceless minority. Hi ! Evolvers of ideas !

HITLER : My leader . . . perhaps. . . . Don't trouble. I've already got a slogan : anti-Semitism. (*Bellowing.*) Dirty Jews ! Death to the Jews ! Perish Judah ! And so on, in endless variations.

SATAN : Excellent.

GENERAL STAFF : Worthy of the Fuehrer.

ALL DEVILS : Hear, hear. (*They emit a whining chuckle.*)

SATAN : And now a gesture, something to show

54

that you all belong, something tiring and silly, but theatrical, so that the masses should automatically adopt it . . . something dynamic. Hi! Movement experts!

HITLER: I have an idea, my Fuehrer—— (*Raises arm, as though to request a hearing.*)

SATAN (*interrupting*): The very thing! A fine gesture. We don't want anything else. And as to the words of salutation——

RUNTY (*bounds forward with Hitler salute*): Heil Hitler! Sieg Heil!

GENERAL STAFF (*with raised arms*): Heil Hitler! Sieg Heil!

ALL DEVILS (*neigh-laugh madly*).

SATAN (*takes step forward; somewhat tired, but very satisfied*): You may begin.

Sudden blackout.

CURTAIN.

ACT II

SCENE I

November, 1932. Party meeting at a Berlin stadium. The scene represents the rear of the platform, which is about 6 feet high. The ornate steps leading onto the platform are right in the Centre. On the right, arm-chairs upholstered in red plush.

Beyond the platform, at the back, a grey valance hung in a semicircle is visible. Beyond and below this is the imaginary auditorium, facing the invisible front of the platform. The movement, murmur or rhythmic shouts of the invisible audience are heard according to the presumed progress of the meeting.

At the rise of the curtain the GENERAL STAFF *are discovered sitting in the chairs.* HITLER *is sitting apart from and facing them, and the audience, at right centre. From the invisible auditorium comes a chorus of long-drawn " Sieg-Heil," repeated three times. The bawls merge into a quiet but continuous buzz, which persists throughout the scene, until* HITLER *ascends to the platform.* GOERING *is coming down the steps, obviously exhausted with the effort of oratory. He comes slowly, with clumsy movements ; his hair is dank, his face covered with perspiration. He sits down among the others, wiping his brow.*

The others are talking in a low voice, now and then throwing anxious glances towards HITLER, *who sits in a brooding attitude.*

GOEBBELS (*suddenly rises, says something in low, excited tones to the others, then ups to the Fuehrer*) : Mein Fuehrer, you're to speak after the interval.

HITLER (*remains motionless, as though he had not heard*).

GOEBBELS : Mein Fuehrer, you're to speak in ten minutes. (*Bends closer, low but incisive.*) Pull yourself together ! You can't keep the Party in good heart like this, or keep a hold on the masses. You must speak in ten minutes—pull yourself together !

HITLER (*looks up ; in a weary, crushed manner*) : Yes, I'll speak . . . in ten minutes. But all's lost, Goebbels, we're finished.

GOEBBELS (*energetic*) : Nothing's lost, mein Fuehrer.

GOERING (*rises, throws a jealous look towards the two, then quickly ups to them*) : How did you like my speech ? (*No reply.*) What is it, Goebbels ?

HITLER (*as above*) : Everything's lost. Why should I speak ? What's the use ?

GOEBBELS (*now somewhat irritable*) : Mein Fuehrer, there's a crowd of nine thousand people in the hall——

GOERING (*zealously*) : And they're waiting to hear you, mein Fuehrer.

HITLER (*hysterical outburst*) : Nine thousand ! That's just it ! Why not twenty thousand ? Why not thirty thousand or fifty thousand as in the past ? Nine thousand ! You didn't even dare to hire a big place. You know best that everything's lost.

GOEBBELS : How can you talk like that, mein Fuehrer ! Nine thousand Party members, the pick of your old followers——

HITLER (*breaking in, roughly*) : Party members ! I don't care a damn for them ! I want the masses, the German people, millions of new people, not a few thousand (*contemptuous*) old Party members ! We've got *them* already. Yes, that's all you can do, Goebbels —bring along the Party, (*snarling*) make a circus show. (*Raving.*) But see what happened at the elections. On the thirty-first July I had fourteen million voters and now, on the sixth November, I had scarcely twelve million. (*Rises, turning upon* GOEBBELS.) What've you done with the two million votes? What've you done with the movement in these decisive three months? (*Turning towards the others, bawling.*) Answer me! You're all responsible.

ALL *suddenly rise, walk up to the three and line up in a semicircle.*

GOERING : Mein Fuehrer, you can't blame us. We've done everything possible.

HESS : You must get round the old half-wit, mein Fuehrer. You still can't do anything in Germany without Hindenburg.

GOEBBELS : If Hindenburg surrenders only a fraction of his power to us (*large gesture*) we'll see to the rest (*hastily correcting himself*)—you'll see to the rest, mein Fuehrer. But first you must place Hindenburg into the front rank of militant National Socialism.

HITLER (*angry*) : What brilliant advice! Get round him! Place him in the front rank! Can you tell me how I am to approach him? Shall I point to my decreasing vote? To my waning popularity? (*Bawling.*) You've wasted my chances!

HIMMLER (*up to him*) : Let's send the SA into the streets. The march on Berlin!

RIBBENTROP (*advances*) : What about the police? And the Stahlhelm? And the Socialists? And the Communists?

HIMMLER : The night of the long knives must come!

ROEHM : What about the Reichswehr?

GOERING : Schleicher will order them to fire.

HIMMLER : Don't let's wait until we're fired on—
let's fire first.

HITLER (*plaintively*) :   Do you want civil war ?
Which of you's prepared to guarantee that we'd win ?
(*Silence.*) Well, say something. (*Hysterical outburst.*)
It's in the interests of the German people that I should
obtain power without bloodshed. But am I to haggle
with Hindenburg and with every little jack-in-office ?
(*Raving.*) Why is Hindenburg still alive ? Why is
Duesterberg still alive ? Why is Schleicher still alive ?
Why are the Socialist and Communist leaders still
alive ?

GOERING (*cautiously*) :   A word from you, mein
Fuehrer . . . if you give the order . . . those concerned will act. (*Quickly.*) But you don't want civil
war, mein Fuehrer.

HITLER : You mean I'm a coward ! (*Hysterically.*)
I'm not a coward ! (*Slapping the Iron Cross on his chest.*)
I wasn't given this for cowardice. Those who got this
were not afraid for their skins—they were ready to face
death. But I don't want to shed German blood. . . .
How can I be sure I'll win ? (*Cautiously.*) Our race is
too valuable to perish in civil war. If you don't
undertake the responsibility——

ROEHM (*interrupting*) : Nonsense, Adolf. There's no
life insurance in war. Don't let's have any illusions
about escaping responsibility. If we go into the streets
again it'll be either one thing or the other. (*Closer to*
HITLER, *fixing him with his eyes.*) I don't identify myself
with these other gentlemen, and when you talk to us
please don't generalise. But I don't deserve any
reproach, either. I undertook the responsibility and
would have gone on taking it. It was not me who fell
on his belly at the first shot in Munich, in 'twenty-three.

HITLER (*amazed, reproachful*) : Ernst ! what are you saying ? (*Sudden rage.*) I won't tolerate your tone !

ROEHM (*unperturbed*) : It wasn't I who did a bunk when the fight became hot. I want to get that understood once more. If it had depended on me we'd have been in power by now.

HITLER (*gives a start at the words " we'd have been in power "*).

ROEHM (*continuing*) : I'm still prepared to take any responsibility. But they (*indicating the others*) and you yourself, you're too weak. Two million votes one way or another—what does it matter ? Who cares about the voters and about the whole bag of tricks once we've got the power ? I've got half a million SA men in arms !

HIMMLER (*enthusiastic, vying*) : And I've got two hundred thousand SS men, they're worth at least——

ROEHM (*turns to* HIMMLER ; *belligerently*) : What ? At least what is your SS worth ?

HIMMLER (*facing him, no less belligerently*) : At least as much as—— (*Thinks better of it.*) I say, Roehm, why do you keep baiting me ?

ROEHM (*coldly*) : I don't bait my subordinates. I call them to account. (*Menacingly.*) And I'll make a note of it, Himmler.

HIMMLER (*darkly*) : So will I, Roehm.

GOEBBELS : Gentlemen . . . we've no time to quarrel over personal vanities. What is at stake is that power——

HITLER (*hysterically*) : Power, power ! Why, even my popularity's in danger. You've lost it for me. To-day it's the masses, the voters, the people who're deserting me, to-morrow it'll be the Party, then my friends . . . or perhaps my friends first. Each of you

considers his own petty affairs more important than
me and the movement.

GOERING : That's a hallucination, mein Fuehrer.
It's impossible to desert Adolf Hitler—the Cause—the
Party.

HITLER : Desert or sell me, betray the Cause and the
Party. . . . (*Bawling*.) The Party will rot and dissolve
by itself. If things go on like this it won't be power
I shall be taking over one day, but . . . but we might's
well make our getaway at once. (*In despair*.) Goebbels
reports that people are grumbling, the leaders vacillating,
I see you're quarrelling among yourselves, and the
money's melting away. (*Hysterically*.) What about
money ? The Party has a debt of nearly a thousand
million marks. (*A moment's shocked silence*.)

GOERING (*to* GOEBBELS, *low, reproachful*) : Did you
have to——

HITLER (*turns hysterically on* GOERING) : Did he have
to what ? Do you want to keep something secret
from me ? Do you want to hide something or lie
to me ?

GOERING (*embarrassed*) : Mein Fuehrer, we know
that practically the whole of the money was spent on
propaganda.

GOEBBELS (*irritably*) : Yes, practically the whole !
Salaries, rewards, motor-cars and (*ironically*) full-dress
uniforms cost nothing, what ? And if I didn't do the
propaganda, dear Goering, you wouldn't have been
able to collect even what little you have collected
with so much difficulty. Getting the money's your
task, dear Goering, but you haven't performed what
you undertook to do. The few hundred millions from
heavy industry was nothing. You could've got ten
times more if you'd made them understand what is at

stake. But you allowed yourself to be paid off with a little small change.

GOERING (*aggressively*) : This is a veiled accusation, if I understand you aright ?

GOEBBELS (*ignores this, continuing*) : I've hardly been able to send anything abroad. It's a shame. The entire world press is bellowing against us, and we haven't got even three papers in foreign countries. I send them a thousand marks every now and then, instead of buying a thousand newspapers, as we ought. There's no money ! I've been obliged to send the SA into the streets—not to fight, but to shake a collecting box under people's noses, like so many Jewish charity collectors. Yes, the SA ! (*Imitating the collectors' banter.*) " Help the naughty Nazis ! " The boys had to make up to people into whom they'd rather have stuck their knives. But if they hadn't collected a little money before the election——

HITLER (*as though just realising*) : What ? The SA and street collections ? What about the heavy industries ? The banks ? The large estates ?

GOERING (*clumsily defensive*) : Unfortunately, mein Fuehrer, they're still vacillating—under the influence of the Jews and the priests.

HITLER (*bawling*) : That's no excuse ! If they were willing I shouldn't need you to convert them. It's your task to wrest them away from the power of others. You have failed ! (*Raving.*) And what about the Reichswehr ? Why is it that the Reichswehr is not yet in my camp ?

HESS (*trying to calm him*) : You know very well, mein Fuehrer, that we must go gently with the Army. Of course, the organisation of the Army is proceeding. Our men are there in every regiment.

HITLER : They are—and Schleicher's going to attend to them. (*Hysterically.*) That's where you ought to've started—with the Army. To make sure they don't resist when we go out into the streets. But to-day . . . I don't think I can be sure of my own party.

ROEHM (*low, hard*): Don't talk like an old woman, Adolf. Don't deliver yourself to them . . . don't betray your weakness.

HITLER (*stares at him, outburst*): Can I no longer trust my own men ? The men I raised——

ALL (*except* ROEHM, *in a chorus of protest*) : Mein Fuehrer ! . . .

HITLER : And all you could get together is nine thousand people. And you expect me to step in front of them and talk to them of victory. (*Suddenly crushed.*) It's no use. We're finished, we're finished.

STREICHER (*elbows his way to the front*): Mein Fuehrer, the situation's not exactly rosy, but you mustn't despair—everyone has difficulties. (*The half-wit.*) I'll publish some juicy ritual murder in the next number of the *Stuermer*. (*Preening himself.*) The usual story, you know, it always gets them. Three Jews kidnap a German girl, assault her, murder her and——

RIBBENTROP (*very irritably*): That'll do, Streicher. (*To* HITLER.) Mein Fuehrer, I told you, did I not, that unless the Party comes out with a positive foreign political programme before the elections there was going to be trouble. (*With emphasis.*) Friendship with Britain. (*Vehemently.*) I hate Britain. But do you think, gentlemen, British public opinion played no part in directing the temper of the voters and in the result of the elections ? And do you think we couldn't win the whole of British public opinion, with the exception of the Jews and the Labour Party, to our

63

side if we made friendly overtures to Britain ? (*Sharply.*) They're afraid of us, therefore they desire our friendship. One must know how to talk to them.

GOEBBELS (*wave of the hand*): I don't care a damn for Britain. I don't desire the friendship of a corpse.

RIBBENTROP : Your business is propaganda, Goebbels, not foreign policy.

GOEBBELS (*peevish*): But it's no use your having a foreign policy, dear Ribbentrop, without my propaganda, without my work in foreign countries.

HITLER (*raving*): How dare you quarrel in my presence ! (*The others jerk themselves to " attention."*) It is I who make both internal and foreign policy. (*Sudden uncertainty.*) We must save the situation . . . the Party, the movement. (*Sudden fit, he bangs the back of the chair.*) Somebody must answer for every failure. Schleicher's in power and he may dissolve the Party within a week and hang every one of you. Goering, you'll hang. Himmler, you'll hang. Every one of you will hang, diplomats and propaganda chiefs and all— because you've missed your opportunity. I want to obtain power by constitutional means, I want a majority, then I'll turn everything upside down, but I won't take any risks until I've got complete power—— (*Breaks off, stares in front of him, fresh outburst.*) But you've robbed me of the chance ! Are we going to march, what ? And what happens to us if we fail ? I meant to leave the bloodshed for the time when I had the power—in case someone wanted to take it from me—there'd be civil war then ! (*Coldly, objectively.*) I want the people, but I also want the capitalists —why didn't you get the lot of them ? You allowed them to haggle with you, to fling you a few hundred millions—you let Hugenberg and the other scoundrels do that, and now they're driving us into a corner. Do they want me to get their chestnuts out of the fire for them? To destroy Communism, break the workers, then become a member of the board at Krupps or the Farben-Industrie? (*Bawling.*) I want Germany, I want full power. It's your fault if I can't get it. (*Seizes* GOEBBELS *by the lapels of his coat.*) Your propaganda's rubbish! (*Turns to* GOERING, *shakes him by the shoulder.*) Where's our power, Goering! And you others. . . . Bunglers, cowards, selfish fools that you are—you've lost me all I've built up. I myself will go to the industrialists, the bankers, the Junkers, the priests—I, Adolf Hitler, Fuehrer of the National Socialist Party— and its commercial traveller. . . . (*Suddenly collapses, crashes into his chair with his head lolling.*) We're finished. We're finished. (*Hysterical sobs.*)

GENERAL STAFF (*stand perplexed, looking down at the Fuehrer*).

> During the above the noise from the imaginary auditorium has been gradually increasing.

GOEBBELS (*sudden energy*): This can't go on. (*Consults watch.*) Three minutes late! We either carry on or we must drop the whole thing.

GENERAL STAFF (*stand looking at the Fuehrer, then eye each other with mutual hatred*).

ROEHM: This is what Horst Wessel died a martyr's death for.

GOERING (*significantly*): This is what we've burned all our bridges for.

RIBBENTROP (*low*): Speak for yourself.

> Brief silence.

GOEBBELS (*suddenly ups to* HITLER, *taps him on the*

E   65

shoulder): Mein Fuehrer! Pull yourself together. There's nothing wrong, is there? (*Low, incisive.*) Remember your oath. . . .

HITLER (*jerks his head up, stares at* GOEBBELS).

GOEBBELS (*continuing, louder*): . . . to the German people.

HITLER (*rises with moonstruck expression*): My oath . . . to the German people. . . . (*As though coming to his senses.*) My oath. (*Lucidly.*) My aims. My desires. My duty. My interest. (*Shakes himself, advances; his whole bearing is changed; for a moment he fixes the audience with a hypnotic—and hypnotised—stare, then suddenly turns round and, pushing the others aside, mounts the steps.*)

GOEBBELS (*quickly joins him*): One moment, mein Fuehrer. I must speak first—to introduce you.

HITLER (*half turning on the third step*): Not to-night. (*He hurries onto the platform, stands with his back to the audience and facing the invisible audience. Vociferous, "*Heil Hitler!*" He stands with his right arm extended, then, with his left, he motions his hearers to silence. In the instantaneously dead stillness he starts to speak. His voice, at first low, is reproduced by a dozen loudspeakers in the hall beyond.*) Party members, German fellow-countrymen and women, I salute the fifty thousand German martial spirits who have come here to-night to hear the truth. (*Brief pause.*) The elections are over. Those who read the result not from paper, but from the hearts of the German people (*from here his voice rises, until it finally becomes a hysterical screech*), will realise that they have ended in smashing victory for National Socialism. There were a few dozen traitors, intimidated people and Jew-retainers who deserted us—but what do they matter? What does it matter that the Jewish Bolshevik agitators and the Jewish capitalist press are screaming their stupid lies about the defeat of Adolf Hitler? It matters nothing. There are sixty million Germans who regard me as their leader. (*His voice is drowned by a thunderous* " Heil Hitler ! ", *repeated. The* GENERAL STAFF, *at the rear and below the platform, stand stiffly at attention.*)

QUICK CURTAIN.

But the clamour is still audible, until it gradually merges into a low buzz, as though of distant voices in conversation.

SCENE II

27th February, 1933. One of the officers' rooms at a Berlin
SA barracks. Wide bench and a few chairs along
the right wall. Long table, chairs, in centre. Two
windows in back wall, between them a portrait of the
Fuehrer, with the inscription : " Ein Volk, ein Reich,
ein Fuehrer ! " Door in downstage end of right wall.
Rack with overcoats at downstage end of left wall.
More pegs over bench, with gun holsters, daggers, etc.,
suspended from them.

A number of SA officers are sitting round the table.
Some are half dressed, others in full uniform. Mugs
of beer on the table.

HEINZ (*sub-groupleader, continuing his tale*): . . . he
trembled as only a Jew can tremble. (*Imitating.*) " I
haven't done anything wrong, Herr Sturmfuehrer "
. . . (*Guffaw from the others.*) Herr Sturmfuehrer ! So
I say to him : Ah, you dirty Jew, now I'm Herr
Sturmfuehrer, but before we came into power you
called me a hooligan, a gangster, a bandit, eh ? He
went green in the face, literally green. Then his son
came up, a pigeon-chested Jew-brat, and he sez, " Mein
Herr, let's talk sense. We haven't done anything
wrong, but we're prepared to make certain sacrifices
in order to be left alone." Of course, I twigged at
once. So I sez to him, Izzy, what do you mean by
sense ? So he sez, " cash." So I sez that's a bit of
all right, as if I wanted to agree. How much, I sez ?
So he goes to the desk and gets out a note for a
thousand. I sez let me have it, and he gives it to me.

68

(*Extracts note from pocket and waves it.*) Then the Jew-brat sez, " Will you leave us alone now ? " Of course, I sez, and (*demonstrating*) I give him a good wallop. Crack ! He folded up at once. The old Jew screamed, his wife screamed. Smack ! Bang ! and down they went. Then I called the boys from the staircase : Wash up, tidy up and bring them in. (*Uproarious guffaws.*) I'll show them, the damned Jews, trying to bribe us. No fear. They can't bribe us.

KUNZ (*sub-groupleader, interested*) : But you've got the cash, Heinz.

HEINZ (*surprised*) : Well, why not ?

KUNZ : You said they can't bribe us.

HEINZ : They can't ! I beat them and had them brought in, didn't I ?

KUNZ : But what about the thousand ?

HEINZ (*with profound surprise*) : Why, it belongs to me. I reported to Herr Sturmfuehrer Bottke at once that I'd arrested a family of dirty Jews for trying to bribe me, and I showed him the note and asked what to do with it. So he sez, keep it, you deserve it. (*Guffaws.*)

KUNZ : I wish I could find a Jew with a thousand marks. I'm up to my neck in debt.

HEINZ : You're a fool if you can't find one. All you have to do is to look round, pick out your Jew, pay him a visit with the boys at dawn—and the rest's easy. (*Turns towards portrait on back wall.*) Heil Hitler !

ALL : Heil Hitler ! (*Guffaws.*)

SCHOLZ (*sub-groupleader*) : We faced danger for ten years. We're entitled to get something out of it now.

BINZ (*sub-groupleader*) : Well, I don't mind telling you, boys, I could do with a bit of mazumah myself.

But not merely in the way of occasional windfalls. I'd like a good, fat job.

LIEDTKE (*same rank*): That'll come. We're only at the beginning. But my brother-in-law's already got something. He had a Jewish . . . acquaintance, a man he knew by sight, you know, first saw him in the café, you know, in the old days. Well, this fellow called on him and asked him to become a partner in his business, in name only, of course, not to do any work, and he offered him three thousand a month. My brother-in-law accepted—why not? There's nothing wrong in taking the money from the Jew. Besides, my brother-in-law says he'll wait a few months, then kick the Jew out of his own shop. (*Guffaws.*) Don't worry, there are good times coming.

TIEDCKE (*same rank*): I had a case, too, though I wasn't quite so lucky as Heinz. It was the day before yesterday. I got on a tram and there was a fat Jewess sitting close by the entrance. I'm going to have some fun, I said to myself. Get up! I say to the Jewess. She looked at me stupidly, as if she didn't understand. So I said: I'm speaking to you, Rebecca! (*Guffaws.*) All the passengers laughed like mad. If you see a uniform, stand up, I went on at the Jewess. So she heaved herself up. Then a civilian, an Aryan German, called out: "All Jews get off the tram!" You should've seen how they hared it!

WILKE (*same rank*): I had a similar experience the other day. Me and the boys chased about a hundred Jews out of a café in the Friedrichstrasse. (*Bawling.*) All Jews get out! (*Normal voice.*) They ran like hares. They even left their overcoats. Somehow, I saw a silver fox tie fall at my feet, I couldn't tell to whom it belonged, so I picked it up and took it away. I gave it to my Grete. (*Guffaws.*) But I'd rather do a little visiting at dawn. (*Guffaws.*)

BULKE (*same rank*) : I kicked about two dozen Jews out of a cinema the other day. (*Dreamily.*) But it isn't the real thing. Well . . . they'll be sending us out into the streets one day soon. Then we shan't only be singing about the night of the long knives.

HEINZ : You know, when I was in the same group with Horst Wessel we got an order one night to go out and pick a quarrel with the Communists in the street. They were holding a procession of some kind.

KUNZ (*reverently*) : You knew Horst Wessel personally ?

HEINZ : Knew him ! He was my pal. I was there when he fell.

SCHOLZ : Say, Heinz, someone once told me it wasn't the Communists that killed him.

HEINZ : Who told you that ? It was the Communists.

SCHOLZ : Well, I believe you.

HEINZ (*reflective*) : We must say it was the Communists.

BINZ : What do you mean—we must say so ?

HEINZ (*uncertainly*) : We got to say so. That's what people must think. (*Brief pause.*) But I was with him at the time. (*Suddenly, low.*) Listen, boys, I'll tell you what really happened. It won't hurt if you know the truth, but (*finger on lips*) . . . otherwise . . . (*grips his dagger*).

LIEDTKE : You can trust us, Heinz.

HEINZ : Well, all right then. Well—there was no street fight. We were sitting in a tavern . . . (*seized with the narrator's élan*) and the girls from the street and the surrounding houses began to come in. Horst took a fancy to one of them and he started to wink at her and the whore winked back, although she had a fellow sitting with her, so Horst went up to her. So the bully gets up, he was properly soaked, he was, and he sez to Horst, go away and play, little boy. He was a big fellow, Ali Hoehler his name was, a bully, everybody knew him down there. So Horst he slinks back to his table and sez he won't start anything with a drunken swine. But he goes on staring at the street walker and she keeps on looking at us, then she gets up slowly and walks past our table wiggling her behind towards Horst. I say, Karl, sez Horst, I like this bitch a lot, and just look at her bully, he's out to the world. In fact, the fellow had his head on the table as if he was asleep. Well, so Horst gets up and follows the whore out of the bar parlour into the street. Then suddenly her bully jumps up, looks round for the girl, and of course she isn't there. So he dashes out into the street. Phew! I sez to myself, there's going to be a fight, so I hurry after him. But I couldn't see them nowhere. Where the blazes could they've got to, I sez to myself. Well, I sez, Horst must've taken the girl to his digs, and Hoehler's gone after them. Well, I sez to myself, he's in for it, he is, and I ran to Horst's place as fast as I could. But I was too late. There they were rolling on the floor. Of course, I wanted to help Horst, but before I knew where I was he gives a scream . . . it was bloody awful I can tell you . . . then Ali he picks himself up, but Horst he lies still. Then Ali staggers out of the room, and I kneel down over Horst—there was a long knife sticking out of his chest. It gave me such a turn I let out such a yell. . . . Then a lot of people crowded into the room and someone sent for an ambu-

lance. By then the boys from the tavern were all
there. The ambulance took Horst away, and I and the
boys went to the post to report. Well, the Ober-
sturmtruppfuehrer said, well, comrades, this is a fine
mess. We must report it to the Fuehrer himself.
Listen carefully, Sub-groupleader Heinz. You and the
other five comrades here make a blood bond here and
now and swear on the honour of Horst Wessel that
you'd keep your mouths shut. What happened was
not *this*. You fought with a group of Communists
and . . . you understand? Of course I understand,
sez I. So we were agreed. Of course, they made a
terrible to do about it. Adolf himself went to the hospital several times to see Horst, and our papers wrote
that Horst was the martyr of National Socialism, he
was stabbed to death by Communists in a street fight.
Poor Horst held on for a few months, then he kicked
the bucket. And what d'you think happened to Ali?
He was copped the day after the knifing, because of
course everybody knew who done it. He didn't deny
it neither. Serve him bloody well right, that's what
he said. Well, Ali got seven years then (*sarcastically*)
and a posh trial it was, too. Seven years for man-
slaughter—that's what the judge give him. We give
him something else. The other day we went to
the prison, fifty of us . . . (*bawling*). We want Ali
Hoehler! The Governor didn't make no fuss. (*Low.*)
We had Goering's order. (*Violent tone.*) Doing his
time, was he? Under the protection of the law, was
he? Well, we took him under our protection, yes, sir.
Outside the prison, in the field. (*Low, bloodthirsty.*)
He got his all right. All we left was a bundle of bloody
rags. . . . (*Low.*) That's how it happened. Only . . .
(*finger on lips*) this is in strict confidence, you know.

WILKE : We'll keep mum all right.

BULKE : It's incredible.

HEINZ : You know, sometimes it makes me laugh to think that if I'd taken a fancy to that bitch, then you'd be singing not the Horst Wessel song but the Karl Heinz song.

ALL (*guffaw, then sing in chorus the concluding verse of the Horst Wessel song*).

TIEDCKE : Heil Horst Wessel ! Long live—— (*Breaks off as door is flung wide open.*)

BOTTKE (*group leader, hastens into the room ; he is in fulldress uniform*) : Get ready ! (*To those in shirt-sleeves.*) Get ready to march !

SEVERAL (*dress with feverish haste*).

OTHERS (*get their guns, daggers, etc.*).

HEINZ (*downstage with* BOTTKE) : What is it, Bottke ? Anything doing ?

BOTTKE : So it seems.

HEINZ : Don't be so abrupt, Bottke. What's happening ?

BOTTKE : You'll know in time, Untersturmtrupp-fuehrer Heinz.

HEINZ (*taken aback*) : Stop larking, Kurt.

BOTTKE : Silence.

HEINZ : You be careful, Kurt. Better not fall out with me. Any man whose brother has done a bunk to Vienna with the important files of the Socialists and taken a job there under the Reds can't afford——

BOTTKE (*startled gesture to stop*).

HEINZ : I'll keep quiet, you know that, although those letters that I found at your brother's lodgings—— (*Sudden consuming curiosity.*) Won't you tell me, Kurt ? Are we going out into the street ?

BOTTKE (*with difficulty*) : Yes, we are.   But please, Karl, no more questions.

HEINZ (*excited*) : A pogrom ?

BOTTKE (*as above*) : Not yet.

HEINZ : What then ?   Surely you can tell me ?   I suppose you know everything.

BOTTKE (*tormented*) : I don't know anything.

HEINZ : Shall I ask your brother in Vienna ?

BOTTKE : You're killing me, you bastard.   I don't know anything. . . . I only heard . . . from the chief sturmfuehrer . . . and he heard at headquarters . . . from Goering's adjutant, he says. . . .

HEINZ (*burning curiosity*) : What ?

BOTTKE : We're going all out.   Smash the Communists and Socialists.   Bust up all the parties.   We must make sure of the election on the fifth of March. The Fuehrer wants a hundred per cent. . . . He will seize power completely.   There's going to be a dictatorship.

HEINZ (*enthusiastic*) : A putsch !   To-night ?

BOTTKE (*painfully*) : A putsch. . . . But it'll be the Communists who'll plan a putsch and . . . the Reichstag will be burnt down.

HEINZ (*angrily*) : Dirty Communists !   Are we going to prevent it ?

BOTTKE (*as above*) : No, we aren't. . . . I mean, it won't be the Communists. . . . I mean . . . (*In a whisper.*) Don't you understand, you fool ?   We'll do the firing.   Goering's men are already there.   They'll set fire to the Reichstag and that will be the signal for us to go out into the street and . . . you understand ?

HEINZ (*delighted*) : Magnificent !

BOTTKE : But I warn you, Karl—not a word to anyone. Otherwise . . . (*Draws finger across his throat.*)

The others are now ready and have collected by the windows.

BOTTKE : Comrades ! (*The sub-groupleaders stand at attention.*) Go and get your groups ready. In ten minutes you line them up in the square and wait for the alarm. With the alarm, each group will receive its orders where to go and what to do.

Distant murmur off, growing stronger. A pale glow penetrates through the windows, gradually developing into a suffused red radiance—it is the reflection of a big fire.

BOTTKE : SA officers, the Fuehrer is entrusting you to-night with a great task. (*Exit.*)

The windows reflect a flare-up.

HEINZ (*bursting with the news, goes up to the others, while* BOTTKE *is engaged with the others, draws* KUNZ *to the front*) : You know what's up, boys ? I'll tell you— but keep mum. (*Low.*) To-night Goering's going to——

Door crashes open.

SA COMMANDER (*in the doorway*) : The Reichstag is on fire. The Communists have fired it. Adolf Hitler's going to smite his enemies to-night. Forward !

HEINZ (*facing the sub-groupleaders*) : Forward march ! Heil Hitler !

ALL (*with raised arms*) : Heil Hitler ! (*All tramp out of the room.*)

QUICK CURTAIN.

Scene III

Autumn, 1933. At the rise of the curtain the stage is in darkness, with a back-cloth screening the back. Sudden spotlight on the right, downstage.

HITLER (*in the spotlight, in party uniform ; speaking quietly, not oratorically, as though thinking aloud*) : First, the Jews. Then the Catholic Church. Then all the other churches. Then the priesthood, as a whole, and all religion. Then the so-called aristocracy of birth and wealth. Then the middle class, (*sarcastically*) particularly the intellectuals. First in Germany, then (*sweeping gesture*) abroad, everywhere. All the nations, white and black, all the continents, all the oceans. (*Bawling.*) But first the Jews !

> *The spotlight is extinguished for a moment, then darts to another part of the stage.*

GOEBBELS (*in the spotlight, in uniform ; in a cold, intelligent, explanatory tone*) : Germany's misfortune, the plague of the world, are the Jews. They are poisoners, destroyers. They are corrupters of culture, putrefactors of civilisation. I will eradicate them from German science and art, I will stamp out their very memory from German cultural life.

> *The spotlight is extinguished for a moment, then darts to another point.*

GOERING (*in a coarse voice*) : The cause of the shame and disgrace of the German people are the Jews. It was they who stabbed in the back the indomitable German front in the West in nineteen-eighteen. It was they who betrayed the German ideal and the German cause. It was they who grew fat on the misery of the

German people. It was they who had the gold, we who had the misery. Jewish capital and Jewish Bolshevism combined to destroy Germany and annihilate the German people. I will extirpate the Jews from German economic life.

The spotlight after a moment appears at another point.

LEY (*drunken bawl*): The Jews have sucked the German worker dry, while the Jewish worker engaged in sabotage and lived like a count. There's no room for Jews among German employers or workers. I will extirpate the Jews from German labour.

The spotlight reappears elsewhere.

STREICHER (*barking*): They bake their ritual cake with the blood of innocent children and young virgins. They rape your daughters, seduce your wives, pollute your pure German Aryan blood. One ritual murder after another. One case of race pollution after another. With their spirit, their money, their power, their occult forces, they are murdering the German people, the entire German race. How long are we going to stand it? Death to the Jews! *Deutschland erwache!* Perish, Juda!

The spotlight is snuffed out. The back-cloth is raised. We see part of a street in a German provincial town. A row of houses from extreme upstage right to extreme downstage left, with pavement and part of the roadway. At extreme upstage right, a crossing represented in perspective. There are shops in the ground floor of the houses. Three of them, not adjacent, bear on doors and windows, in red paint and coarse characters, the word " JUDE." Distant noise from the end of the street.

A THIN WOMAN (*emerges from one of the Jewish shops, looks towards the end of the street*): Good gracious!

78

A FAT WOMAN (*leaning out of a window above the shop*) : What is it, Martha ?

THE THIN WOMAN : They're coming. (*Runs through house door near shop entrance.*)

THE FAT WOMAN (*quickly shuts window, draws blind*).

A MAN (*comes from another shop*) : What's all this noise ?

ANOTHER MAN (*comes running from the end of the street*) : They're coming !

OTHERS (*appearing in doorways and at windows*) : What is it ? What's all the shouting ? What's happened ?

PEDESTRIANS (*come hurrying from right*) : The SA are coming ! (*They hurry out into the imagined continuation of the street downstage left.*)

> *Terrified men and women dash out of the shops, hastily put up shutters, carry away exhibited goods.*

SEVERAL PEOPLE (*leaning out of windows and gazing towards right*) : They're coming ! They've just turned the corner !

AN OLD WOMAN (*with dishevelled hair, in window*) : Police ! Police !

AN OLD MAN (*in another window*) : Phone the . . . the fire brigade ! (*Vanishes.*)

> *The stage is now empty and frozen into immobile silence. The noise approaches and crystallises into the rhythmic tramp of many feet.*
>
> *At the extreme right a storm troop forming twos appears. The men, led by two group leaders, enter at a slow pace.*

FIRST LEADER (*stops in front of the first Jewish shop, banging the shutter with his fist*) : Open ! Open !

SECOND LEADER (*stops in front of first house door*) :
Six men into the house. Forward march !

FIRST LEADER (*kicks at shutter*) : Open or I'll smash
it in.

> *The shutter is slowly, painfully rolled up from the
> inside.*

A PALE-FACED WOMAN (*appears*) : What can I do
for you, sir ?

FIRST LEADER : This is a Jewish shop, eh ?

THE PALE-FACED WOMAN : We are . . . we're
Jewish.

FIRST LEADER : Dirty Jews ! Out on the pavement,
all of you, in front of the window. Everyone in the
shop !

THE PALE-FACED WOMAN (*staggers into position in front
of window*).

OTHERS (*terrified men and women come staggering out of
the shop and join* PALE-FACED WOMAN).

TWO SA MEN (*come from first house, followed by several
men and women, who stop by the front door*).

> (*Behind a shuttered window on the first floor a scream
> is heard, then a revolver shot. Brief silence.*)

SECOND LEADER (*emerging from the house, speaking over
his shoulder*) : The placards !

SA MAN (*appears from the back of his group with several
squares of cardboard inscribed, "I am a dirty Jew," and provided with a loop of string*) : Here they are, Comrade
Sturmfuehrer.

SECOND LEADER (*to Jews lined up*) : Each of you will
hang one round his neck !

A JEWESS (*trembling*) : Are you t-taking us away ?

SA MAN : Shut up, Jewish whore ! Put on the

placard, all of you! (*Lined-up men and women hastily hang placards round their necks.*)

FIRST LEADER (*in door of first shop*): This is done. (*Goes to next Jewish shop, bangs on shutter.*) Open up! And come out!

> Door of shop opens instantaneously; several men and women come out with wobbling knees.

FIRST LEADER: Stand in front of the window! Cards on your necks! (*This is done.*)

SECOND LEADER (*before door of second house*): Six men into the house. Forward march! (*The six vanish.*)

A NAZI (*with beard and Party emblem, in the roadway*): That's right. Take them away, straight to the block. They've been exploiting us long enough, the dirty Jews.

A FEMALE VOICE (*from the back*): Ludwig, you ought to be ashamed of yourself.

AN SA MAN (*suddenly turns in the direction of the voice*): Who's that? If you're not careful——

THE NAZI (*accusing*): Quite right! Take her as well. She's my wife! Hobnobs with Jews. I saw her the other day.

SECOND LEADER (*comes from second house with group of frightened people*): Line up along the wall. Cards round your necks! (*This is done.*)

FIRST LEADER (*in a stentorian voice*): Jews, get off the pavement! Form twos in the roadway.

AN OLD MAN: Where are you taking us? . . .

AN SA MAN (*kicks him*): Get on with you!

THE OLD MAN (*stumbles into roadway*).

THE OTHER JEWS (*with bowed heads follow and form twos*).

ANOTHER SA MAN (*bawling at limping man*): Get a move on, you! (*Raises truncheon.*)

A Young Jew : Don't you dare hit him. Can't you see he's lame !

The SA Man (*strikes him with his truncheon ; young man crashes to the ground and lies still*).

First Leader : You'll stay here and await orders. (*He disappears downstage left ; his voice, off*): Another Jew shop. Open up !

Second Leader : Into the next house ! (*Disappears downstage left ; his voice, off*): Six men into the house ; forward march !

> *Silence and immobility for a few seconds. The captives are in the roadway, forming twos. On the edge of the roadway, in single file, are the SA men, ready to march.*

A Male Voice (*off-stage, at a great distance*): At-tention ! Forward march ! (*Noise of marching feet, partly strong and rhythmical, partly shuffling.*)

Another Voice (*off, but closer*): At-ten-tion ! Forward march !

> *Mixed noises, as above, but louder.*

Third Voice (*off, but quite close, directed at those on the stage*): At-ten-tion ! (*All stiffen to attention.*) Forward march ! (*All march, SA men with stiff, goose-stepping tramp, the captives with a shuffle.*)

> *A seemingly endless procession crosses the stage from downstage left to upstage right—men, women, young and old people, all with bowed heads and cards round their necks. Each group of captives is followed by a group of SA men headed by a Leader. At times a voice off is heard commanding " Attention ! " and " Forward march ! " The procession continues in the grey autumn afternoon.*

Slow Curtain.

82

Scene IV

June 30, 1934. *Late evening. Ernst Roehm's villa at a summer resort near Munich. The scene represents a room crowded with a jumble of rich furniture in atrocious taste. At back, huge settee. To the left of it a large drink cabinet ; on it a bust of Hitler. In the left wall a wide window with red plush curtain. In front of it is a desk, with books, papers, telephone, revolving chair. Low upholstered door between drink cabinet and wall. Large double door in right wall. On each side of it there is a low table, with mirror above it.*

At the rise of the curtain ROLF, ROEHM'S *adjutant, is sitting at the desk. There are large five-branched candelabra on the desk and the two low tables, with thick candles burning in them. A huge radio gramophone, to the right of the settee, is playing a tango, the hit of the season.*

The upholstered door opens, and enter :

ROEHM (*stops in the door, looks round with a nervous jerk of his head ; walks to the gramophone and with a brief, impatient movement turns it off ; he wears a heavy brown silk dressing-gown, red silk scarf, blue silk pyjamas, dark brown leather slippers*).

ROLF (*looking up*) : Ernst. . . .

ROEHM (*hoarse voice*) : You know I hate this squeaking.

ROLF (*rises ; he is wearing a queer silken fancy uniform of feminine cut*) : And you know I adore dance music. (*Advances with the characteristic swaying walk of the pederast.*) Are you upset, Ernst ?

ROEHM (*morosely*) : I certainly am. (*Glance towards*

window.) The heat is simply suffocating and you shut yourself in, with the curtains drawn. (*Goes to wall, manipulates electric switch; the room is flooded with a cold, dazzling light from a large ultra-modern chandelier of inartistic globular design*.) Blow out those candles. You know I hate this silly night club illumination.

ROLF (*coaxing*): And you know how I adore it. The lovely yellow, warm candlelight. And dance music—tangos. (*Advances with dance step*.) Goebbels is a fool. Why doesn't he leave jazz alone? Has he nothing better to do? Does he expect us to dance folk dances to the sound of a brass band or a sword dance in honour of the Fuehrer and Wotan, to the tune of the Ride of the Valkyries?

ROEHM (*irritably*): Really, Rolf . . .

ROLF (*up to him, takes his hand*): Ernst . . . I'll put on the Valkyries' Ride, if you like. (*Sings*.) Ta-ra-ra-ree . . . (*Etc.*) Come, let's dance a sword dance—a dagger dance—a revolver dance. (*Suddenly embraces* ROEHM, *who pushes him away with distaste; offended*.) Ernst . . . how unkind you are to me. (*Plaintively*.) Why are you so rude to me?

ROEHM (*his hand involuntarily glides over* ROLF's *chin, arm, hip*): Don't be childish, Rolf.

ROLF: You never used to say not to be childish. Up till now you liked me as I was. (*Scared*.) Are you tired of me? Are you angry with me?

ROEHM (*negative shake of the head*).

ROLF: Can I leave the candles on?

ROEHM (*affirmative nod*).

ROLF: Can I switch off this horrible chandelier? (*Does so*.) Can I leave the window shut? Can I—— (*Very childishly*.) Ernst, may I put on that tango again?

ROEHM (*involuntary laugh*): You're a baby. An ass.

84

(*Suddenly gloomy.*)   You're feeling happy.   I'm not.
(*Goes to desk, rings bell.*)

AN SA ORDERLY (*very young, girlish face, uniform of
feminine cut*): Sir?

ROEHM: I want Adjutant Wolf.   Why hasn't he
come in?

ROLF (*jealous*): What do you want with him?

THE SA ORDERLY: Adjutant Wolf hasn't arrived
yet, sir.

ROEHM (*nervous jerk of the head*): Well, who was it
arrived while I was changing?   I heard a car.

THE SA ORDERLY: It was Adjutant Rolf's tailor
from Munich.

ROLF (*angry*): Why didn't you tell me, then?

THE SA ORDERLY: He said he wanted to get his
patterns ready first.

ROEHM (*after gloomy silence*): As soon as Adjutant
Wolf arrives, send him in.   (*Exit* ORDERLY.)

ROLF (*jealous*): I say, Ernst, what do you want with
Wolf?   Can't you live without him even for one day?
(*Grave.*)   Is anything wrong?   You look so terribly
depressed, Ernst.

ROEHM: Gregor Strasser hasn't come.   He ought
to've arrived in the early evening.

ROLF: He'll arrive in the morning.   Perhaps he had
a breakdown on the road.

ROEHM: And Wolf isn't back yet. . . . (*Paces room
in great agitation.*)   It's nearly midnight.   I can't
understand it.

ROLF (*scared, humble*): What's the matter, Ernst?   I
don't like to see you in this nervous state.   I'm worried
about you.   I'm so sorry for you.   (*Goes to desk, rings.*)

THE SA ORDERLY (*instantaneously appears in door*):
Sir?

85

ROLF : Tell the tailor not to mess about to-night. Give him something to eat and send him off to bed. I'll look at the patterns in the morning. (*Nod towards drink cabinet.*) A drink. (*Low.*) Champagne.

THE SA ORDERLY (*the practised lackey, hastens to cabinet, takes out bottle of champagne, feels whether it is cold enough, removes foil ; slight pop*).

ROEHM (*gives a violent start, looks, turns away*).

THE SA ORDERLY (*places three glasses on large silver tray, pours out, offers tray first to* ROEHM, *then to* ROLF ; *places tray on low table near settee, exit soundlessly*).

ROLF (*timidly, coaxingly*) : Ernst . . . drink my health.

ROEHM (*ignores him, sits on edge of settee, drinks*) : Strasser hasn't come—Wolf hasn't arrived yet. There's something wrong there. (*Irritably.*) Hasn't Strasser sent a message ?

ROLF (*shrug*) : Don't know. Not my business.

ROEHM : He may not have left Berlin at all. I must 'phone him. Is the 'phone in order yet ?

ROLF : Yes.

ROEHM : Has that clicking noise gone ?

ROLF : No, it's still there. But it's nothing. The engineer's examined every instrument, as well as all the lines, right to Munich. He said the click is not a fault. The cables touch somewhere. It's of no importance.

ROEHM : In other words, they're tapping my telephone.

ROLF : You talk like an old woman, Ernst.

ROEHM (*stares at him, is about to say something, but merely waves his hand*).

ROLF : You're so unkind to me, Ernst. (*Refills*

86

glasses.) You must be nice to me. I know you've got to work all day, but in the evening at least——

ROEHM: Don't bother me, boy. (*Drinks up, sits at desk, takes papers from drawer, arranges them with quick, nervous movements, puts one sheaf aside, thinks better of it, tears it up and drops it into the waste-paper basket, but instantaneously bends down and collects the scraps ; hoarsely*): These must be burnt.

Large door suddenly opens.

WOLF (*travel coat over uniform, goggles ; he is tall, broad-shouldered, with energetic movements, yet with something feminine about him ; from doorway*): Ernst, Heydrich didn't come to Munich.

ROEHM (*his face twitching*): Perhaps you simply couldn't find him ?

WOLF: I looked for him everywhere. He didn't put up at the Bayrischer Hof and they knew nothing about him at the Brown House. I waited till six, then I rang his house in Berlin. They said he was still at his office. I rang his office, but there they said he hadn't been since the afternoon and they didn't know where he was.

ROEHM (*beside himself*): I ordered him to come down and he hasn't come! (*Badly perturbed.*) Neither he, nor Strasser. Perhaps he's met with an accident ? (*Pacing the room.*) I don't like Heydrich. . . . The last time he came with the reports I noticed—— (*Suddenly bounds to waste-paper basket and heap of torn paper on desk, grabs them, holds them out to* WOLF.) Burn these.

WOLF (*takes them*): I will. But don't worry about Heydrich. I know him. I'm sure he's got a good reason for not coming. We'll find out in due course.

Nothing wrong with Heydrich. (*Turns to go.*) I'm going to take these things off.

ROEHM (*calls after him*): Come back as soon as you've done so.

ROLF (*jealous*): What do you want with him, Ernst?

ROEHM (*ignores this, paces room, lights chandelier, blows out candles, sits at desk*).

ROLF (*watches him, takes a hesitant step; he would like to remark about the candles, but dare not; goes to gramophone, starts tango, but as* ROEHM *jerks his head, he quickly stops it; plaintively*): You're unkind to me to-night. . . .

WOLF (*returns in uniform, comes close to* ROEHM): But my visit to Munich wasn't wasted. I saw Ludwig and Rupert, I sent a message to Oswald to go to Chiem-See next Sunday instead of Heydrich. (*Noticing* ROEHM's *absent stare.*) You're not listening, Ernst.

ROEHM (*with a start*): Did you burn them?

WOLF: Yes. (*Low.*) You look restless. (*Lower.*) Yet there's no reason. Everything's going to be all right.

ROEHM (*rests his head between his fists, thinking; suddenly rises*): No, it's no good. Before anything can happen, before we do it . . . I must speak with Hitler.

WOLF: What about? We've nothing to talk about with him.

ROEHM: I feel I ought to see him.

WOLF: Then go to prison, what? Or in front of a firing squad. (*Low, incisive.*) You've got nothing to say to that traitor. If you deign to speak with him he'll talk the breath out of your body. You speak with him later, when we've done it—when you can talk with him in safety.

ROEHM: But if anything went wrong . . . if any little detail went wrong——

88

WOLF (*cold assurance*) : We've decided to risk that.
You can't get power for nothing. Only Adolf Hitler
got it for nothing. Only Adolf Hitler avoided, and is
still avoiding, personal risk. Only he wants to be sure
of everything before he moves. Only he refuses to
take the responsibility for anything. He wants others
to risk their skins for him. (*Low, hard.*) What's the
matter with you, Ernst ? Why are you so upset ?

ROEHM (*painfully*) : I don't know. Strasser didn't
come, Heydrich didn't come. There's something
wrong. Have we made a mistake anywhere ?

ROLF (*to* WOLF) : You can't do anything with him,
either, can you ? He's quite crazy to-night.

WOLF : You can't afford these moods, Ernst. Even
if a mistake had been made it doesn't necessarily mean
trouble. A mistake can be made good. (*Significantly.*)
The SA is all right. The Socialists are all right. Otto
Strasser and the Black Front are all right. (*Low.*) Of
course, it was a mistake on your part to upset the
Reichswehr from jealousy about the SA. But you can
rely on Schleicher, and the Reichswehr is in his hands.

ROEHM (*uncertainly, painfully*) : Yes, but . . . if I had
a talk with Adolf——

WOLF (*interrupting*) : You want to get cheated again,
what ? You can't rely on Hitler's word. He's betrayed
our cause, betrayed our Socialism, and he will betray
our Nationalism as well. He's sold himself to the
industrialists, sold himself to the Junkers, the reaction-
aries, the moronic lower middle class. He's sold them
our revolution, the German revolution, he's sold the
German people and——

ROEHM (*interrupting ; in a moonstruck tone*) : If I had
a talk with him and told him to come to his senses
while there's yet time and to come in with us ! Don't

89

let's drop our cause. I'd tell him that things must change at once.

WOLF : You're mad. He'd put you in prison.

ROEHM : I'd tell him that if he'd listen to me I'd bring about the change with him, not against him.

WOLF : Ernst, you're out of your mind. Is that what we've been working for for the past year ? Do you want to ruin everything ?

ROEHM : I'd tell him he's surrounded by thieves——

WOLF (*interrupting*) : Do you think he doesn't know ?

ROEHM : He can't possibly.

WOLF (*cold contempt*) : Really ! He doesn't know what's going on in his glorious Third Reich. Don't be ridiculous, Ernst ! He knows everything, everything's happening with his permission, by his will. Goering's taking seats on one board of directors after another, pocketing millions in fees, royalties and dividends. That's why they don't nationalise the big concerns. He's buying up one block of flats after another, as well as palaces and estates. And what's going to happen to the property of the Jews when it's liquidated ? It'll be acquired by Goering and others of his ilk—if they don't acquire it before. Did you know that he's had the Rembrandts from Dresden sent to his Berlin flat ? How much jewellery he's looted ? How many cars he's got ? And what about Goebbels ? (*Irony.*) The city presented him with a villa. His admirers gave him an estate. He's also been given industrial shares worth hundreds of millions . . . probably by a grateful nation. As to the foreign exchange and securities which he's smuggled abroad, like all the rest of them, I've no idea where he got those, but he's got them, that's the chief thing, he's made provision for himself. The customs don't bother about diplomatic bags, and particularly the personal couriers of Goebbels, Goering, Himmler, Ley, Funk, and all the other bastards. If anything should happen in Germany, there's a private aeroplane in readiness, and then one day an unknown but wealthy someone'll appear in South America. (*Suppressed rage, contempt.*) They're thieves, every one of them. And Hitler doesn't know all this, what? Why, he wants it like that. Let the favourites, the parasites, the sub-leaders grow fat, let them be in with him in the conspiracy. Because let me tell you that Hitler's printing and publishing interests are no trifle. Adolf Hitler, most widely read author in the world, is also the biggest publisher in the world. Splendid, isn't it? It was easy for him to waive his salary as Chancellor. (*Outburst.*) Do you think he doesn't know that there isn't an office in Germany to-day where you could get anything done without a bribe, but that you can get anything at all done with a bribe? Do you think he doesn't know what's going on in the Party, what rivalry, what murderous rivalry, for the fat jobs? He knows everything! He says they've worked for it, fought for it, let them have something out of it. We are fighting for the German people, not in order to fill our bellies and our pockets.

ROLF (*coyly sulky*): What about supper? I'm waiting for you, Ernst, I don't want to eat without you. But I'm terribly hungry. Let's eat. (*Goes to champagne bottle.*)

WOLF: Go to hell! (*To* ROEHM.) What they're doing is not National Socialism but international gangsterism. Don't give in, Ernst! We must clean up the Party and the country. We must save the cause. The Nazi revolution so far has only consisted in kicking the Jews out of their jobs, blackmailing the rich a bit, slaughtering or interning the defenceless—well, our revolution, the real National Socialist Revolution, the Revolution of the Fourth Reich, will be different. But Adolf Hitler's not going to be in it. (*Low, penetrating.*) Captain Ernst Roehm, you can only talk with Hitler when he's standing in front of you, the Fuehrer, with his hands manacled behind his back.

ROEHM (*hypnotised*): Yes. . . . Of course it's intolerable. . . .

WOLF: It's intolerable that Germany's become one vast nest of bandits, that the leaders are worse usurers than the Jews, that the SS and the Gestapo are in the hands of a Himmler!

ROEHM (*carried away*): It's intolerable. . . .

ROLF: I'm intolerably hungry.

WOLF (*rousing* ROEHM): It's intolerable that Ernst Roehm should play a secondary role beside an Adolf Hitler. And even that's uncertain because Hitler's already jealous of you.

> *Noise of large cars drawing up off-stage, then unintelligible talk, the slamming of doors, a brief silence, noise of approaching footsteps.*

ROEHM (*pricks up his ears at the first sounds, now gives a start, goes pale, rises*): What's happening out there?

WOLF: It may be Strasser. (*Goes to window, pulls curtain aside, opens one wing, looks out, jerks his head back; he looks pale; low.*) A whole column of armoured cars.

ROEHM: What the——

> *Large door crashes wide open. Twelve SS men crowd into the room and take up positions with automatics and tommy guns at the ready. The three in the room look terrified.*

THE SS LEADER: Hands up!

ROLF ⎱
WOLF ⎰ (*immediately obey*).

ROEHM (*advances*) : What's the matter, comrade ?

THE SS LEADER : Don't move or we fire.

ROEHM (*stands rigid*).

THE SS LEADER : Hands up, I say.

ROEHM (*slowly raises arms*).

> *Silence. Sound of footsteps from outside.* HITLER
> *appears in the door, with* HIMMLER *and* HEYDRICH
> *behind him.*

HITLER (*looks at the three for a moment*) : The salute
isn't quite right. We Germans salute with the right arm
extended almost horizontally, not with both vertically.

ROEHM (*drops arm lower*) : Heil, mein Fuehrer !

WOLF (*ditto*) : Heil, mein Fuehrer !

ROLF (*dare not move his arms*) : Heil, mein Fuehrer !

HITLER (*jerks his head round, ascertains that he is safe,
advances, takes a queer look at* ROLF, *turns away from him*) :
Umm. " Heil, mein Fuehrer." (*Walks slowly about the
room.*)   A pretty room.   Comfortable, soft, a real
(*irony*) boudoir.   Not exactly the thing for a hard
fighter.   Rather a warm little nest for a couple of
lovers. (*Stares at wide settee.*) A more comfortable
resting-place than an SA camp-bed. Of course, it serves
a different purpose. (*Looking at small table and silver
tray.*)   French champagne. (*Inquiring look over his
shoulder.*)   Where are the oysters ?   The caviar ?   Not
served yet ? (*Comes close to* ROEHM, *fingers sleeve of
dressing-gown.*)   Heavy silk.   Real French or Japanese
make ? (*Turns away, up to* ROLF.) And this . . . this
thing—what is it ?   And its queer uniform.   Heavy
silk again.   Umm.

ROLF (*plaintively*) : Mein Fuehrer . . . I swear . . .
I——

HITLER (*the whining tone angers him*) : Is this the sort of thing you're surrounded with, Roehm ?

ROEHM (*as though* HITLER's *voice had brought him to his senses ; angrily*) : What's this comedy mean, Adolf ?

HITLER (*with lowered head, lugubriously*) : Captain Roehm thinks this is a comedy. (*Snort.*) How dare you talk to me like that, scoundrel ! (*With the assurance of a sleepwalker walks to desk, digs his hand into the papers.*) The papers. The secret reports. The plans. This isn't worth looking at, of course. The interesting part was burnt by Adjutant Wolf half an hour ago. We know. (*Turns on* ROEHM.) A comedy, is it ? I'm not used to putting on comedies. Even a joke's deadly serious to me. Even a farce doesn't make me laugh. (*With emphasis.*) Even when it's about a conspiracy.

WOLF (*turns away contemptuously*).

HITLER (*in a fit of rage*) : Adjutant Wolf ! Stand at attention when you're facing your Fuehrer ! Or with your hands manacled behind you. I trust you like this change of role. (*Ironical courtesy.*) No use your denying it. Even a dead telephone can hear—and even when the receiver is down. And it may carry the words to a record outside, no matter if they're whispered.

ROLF (*imploring*) : Mein Fuehrer . . . I had no part in the conspiracy, I always told Roehm——

HITLER (*frigid irony*) : —that you were hungry. I know. (*Stares at him for a moment, then carries his gaze to* ROEHM.) So these are your friends—nancy boys and (*bawling*) rebels ! One of them incites you to your ruin, the other betrays you at the first sign of trouble.

ROEHM : Adolf . . . I don't know what all this means. You burst in . . . they burst in . . . hands up . . . Is this a Wild West show ?

HITLER (*raving*) : Traitor ! Scoundrel ! Scum !

94

What've you done with my SA? You've infested it with pederasts! You've smuggled it full of homosexuals.

ROEHM: That's a lie.

HITLER: I am lying? Why, you scoundrel, your house is a sink of iniquity.

ROEHM: It's my house. My private life's nothing to you. What you reproach me with now has been no secret. You knew it, but didn't bother about it, indeed, you helped me, protected me, and now you want to use my private life to——

HITLER (*interrupting, raving*): You're the scum of the earth. I don't care a damn for your private life. (*Up to him, looks him up and down.*) You were preparing a revolt against me—against your leader. (*In a paroxysm.*) You were cooking up a revolt against the leader of the German nation, against the greatest German in history! (*Barely articulate.*) Ernst Roehm, you were my friend, my favourite, I entrusted you with great tasks, treated you as my collaborator and wanted to keep you as such—and you betrayed me. I know everything. You thought I wasn't watching you, huh? Every letter you received or wrote, every telephone conversation was known to me—even the whispers in your bedroom came to my ears. (*Snarling.*) No, Ernst Roehm, you're not going to make a blood bath, you're not going to wrest power from me.

ROEHM (*realising that all is lost, recovers himself*): No. You're going to make a blood bath, Adolf. (*Cold irony.*) And you're going to save the Third Reich for Herr Krupp, for the chemical industry, for Goering and the other thieves who've grown too big for you. (*Looking up.*) And for Herr Heydrich, who's betrayed me. (*Gesture.*) You're all worthy of each other.

HEYDRICH (*superior, ironical smile and nod at* ROEHM).

HITLER (*with raised fists and an inarticulate cry bounds towards* ROEHM).

ROEHM : Come on, Adolf, but not with your bare fists, or I'll knock you down.

HITLER (*stops short, low*) : For the sake of your past as a National Socialist fighter I'll have a revolver sent to your cell.

ROEHM (*beside himself*) : I don't want it, Adolf. I'm not going to commit suicide. You must kill me. Shoot me. Stab me to death. (*Bellowing.*) Bring a rope ! I demand that you execute me with your own hands, Adolf Hitler !

HITLER (*shrinks within himself for a moment, forces composure upon himself with an effort*) : Ernst Roehm, I arrest you. (*Gesture.*) Himmler !

HIMMLER : Jawohl, mein Fuehrer. (*To SS men behind him.*) Handcuff him.

FOUR SS MEN (*approach* ROEHM).

WOLF (*screeching*) : Ernst, don't give in !

ROEHM (*bounds back, his hand darts to the pocket of his dressing-gown*).

HITLER (*jerks round ; he is holding a revolver, aiming it at* ROEHM).

ROLF (*drops on his knees, screaming*). Please don't hurt me, please, please. . . . I haven't done anything . . . mein Fuehrer. . . .

WOLF (*two paces behind* ROEHM, *is aiming revolver at* HITLER).

AN SS MAN (*bounds to him, knocks* WOLF'S *hand upwards ; an explosion, crash of glass, the room is plunged into darkness ; shots crash from revolvers, tommy guns*).

CURTAIN.

SCENE V

*The stage is divided into two equal parts by a narrow, two-
foot-high platform running from the front to the back.
It is covered with red plush.   Above it floats a huge
swastika.   Wine-coloured valances, richly folded, right
and left.*

At the rise of the curtain HITLER *is standing on the
platform in a spotlight.   He is in uniform, with the
Iron Cross on his chest, and stands rigid, like a waxwork
figure.   The rest of the stage is in darkness.*

*The figure suddenly comes to life, smiles, gazes at the
audience for a moment, then with an easy movement turns
to face downstage left.*

*At this moment that part of the stage lights up,
revealing, in a row between the platform and the curtains
behind,* PUBLIC OPINION, INTERNATIONAL DIPLO-
MACY, EUROPEAN CIVILISATION, MORALITY, THE
CHURCH, WORLD ECONOMY *and* PEACE.

HITLER (*gazes at the row for a moment, then his right
hand rises in a courteous gesture ; in a charming tone, smil-
ingly*) : But my dear Public Opinion, won't you come
closer ?   Why this timid reserve ?   Indeed, sometimes
there's a shocked, disapproving expression on your face.
Of course, it's those silly crime stories with which a few
sacked Press Jews are feeding you.   (*Friendly.*)   You
needn't be afraid of me, I assure you.   I'm not a cannibal.   Germany's a European country and one of the
guardians of civilisation.   You mustn't be distrustful
with me.   (*Casually.*)   Of course, here at home, within
the Third Reich, there have happened a few unusual
things, but I don't want to force on any foreigner the
things that I like.   Besides, it's our private affair.   (*Some-*

what menacingly.) Everybody's got private affairs, what ?
Well-bred and wise people don't interfere with other
people's private lives. (*Convincingly*.) We Germans are
modest, always have been. Why, all we expect from
you is a little understanding, and as to the world at
large, all we expect is what belongs to us, what we're
entitled to. (*Persuasively*.) It was a German who invented the principle of " live and let live "—a German
poet it was, I don't recollect his name at the moment,
but you probably know it, you're so educated. Why not
look at me in a somewhat friendlier way, my dear Public
Opinion ? That's better. A little smile. . . .

PUBLIC OPINION (*pretty young girl, in bathing costume,
with a wide ribbon inscribed with " Miss Universe " across
her chest, readily steps out of the row and, with a charming,
slightly coquettish smile on her face, performs a ceremonious
bow*) : Why not, Herr Hitler. (*Steps back into row.*)

HITLER : Thank you, Public Opinion. And you,
International Diplomacy. . . . Since I came to power
there's been a strange light in your eyes—the ominous
gleam of persecution mania. Why do you endanger
your health, pray ? After all, it's entirely our own
business how I govern my people and what mode of
life I've created for them. The Germans like it, and
that's the main thing, isn't it ? We really have no right
to pry into each other's . . . shall I say, bedroom secrets.
(*Somewhat menacing*.) Healthy people do not suffer from
nightmares ; wise people don't listen to informers. As
to my dislike of Democracy . . . why, that's a matter
of conviction. After all, it's you who preach freedom of thought. As to my dislike of the Jews . . .
why, that's a matter of taste. For instance, you don't
like the fact that I've left the Palace of Geneva. I
left it chiefly because its style of architecture conflicts

so much with the ancient German style. (*Jovially.*) But sulkiness isn't real anger, is it ; and it's wise to be careful who you're angry with. We don't need to be angry with each other. Let's sit down first at the white table, then at the green table. What's your view of a world anti-Comintern pact ? Or are you more interested in the question of disarmament ? Very well. Let's discuss, make an agreement. Do you want an air pact ? Or a naval pact ? I'm ready for anything—and I make no impossible demands. All I want is a modest little place in the sun. I've no territorial claims. Alsace-Lorraine I leave to the French for ever, the Southern Tyrol and Trieste to my Fascist colleague, Eastern Silesia and Posen to my friends the Poles ; (*sweetly*) my lebensraum lies in a different region, in a region that you yourself don't favour overmuch—in the wild East. (*Indignant tone.*) As far as I'm concerned all the other countries can live and prosper in freedom and independence. As to Britain, there's nothing I could want from her ; the British, after all, are our kith and kin, rich and distinguished relations worthy of emulation. All I want from you, my dear International Diplomacy, is a little goodwill and perhaps one day the handshake of friendship. . . .

INTERNATIONAL DIPLOMACY (*a gentleman with a huge head, in dress-suit and top-hat ; first he tilts his head, as though reflecting, then suddenly steps forward, raises his silk hat with a sweeping gesture*) : We can but try, Fuehrer of Germany ! (*Steps back into row.*)

HITLER : Thank you. What about you, European Civilisation ? Why do you stand so stiffly ? Why do you look so gloomy and downcast ? Apparently you've forgotten about Goethe, Beethoven. (*Protesting gesture.*) Please don't say " that's different." It's true they were not Nazis; on the contrary; but I'm not referring to them in relation to me—in fact, I confess, I have never had any love for them—but in relation to you: you couldn't exist without them, could you? Well, then. That's why, for the sake of the past, I ask for a little confidence, a little patience—patience with me in particular. (*With modest candour.*) You see, I am not educated. But I needed and still need my energies for other things—for action, not for knowledge. (*Narrative tone.*) Politics is not your cup of tea, and the book I wrote is a political work, (*apologetic*) which may excuse its loose style, by the way, but you may nevertheless have read my modest effort, the story of my struggle . . . and you may know the passage where I say there are those who create you, those who carry you, and those who destroy you. Surely it cannot hurt you if I persecute the destructive element. You say we differ as to who is the destructive element? Well, I'll convince you! On the other hand, we Germans have always enriched you and appreciated you, though, of course, in our own way. It would be a pity to raise the question which of us could exist without the other . . . and it would be a thousand pities to exacerbate the matter. So I only ask for one thing—for the present. Please don't let there be any more talk about " German barbarism " or " furor teutonicus." It's time you refused to be taken in by the whisperings of the well poisoners. You speak of the burning of books? Of the fact that I've destroyed pictures, sculptures and other cultural assets? That I've fixed arbitrarily the direction of and set limits to culture? That's only appearances. I've only destroyed and banned that which is bad, ugly and harmful—in my opinion. Actually, I'm mad on all real culture, all real beauty, philosophy, science, literature,

art. . . . I myself have an inkling of the art of painting.
. . . I love the theatre and music. Wagner! *The
Merry Widow*! Sooner or later, my dear European
Civilisation, we'll come to understand each other,
(*menacing*) won't we?

EUROPEAN CIVILISATION (*man with white beard, weary
expression, in black gown and Wagnerian beret, has bundle of
books on shoulder, a lyre in his right, palette and brush in his
left; he steps forward, performs a clumsy, sweeping bow*):
Let's hope for the best, Herr Chancellor! (*Steps back.*)

HITLER: Thank you. (*Friendly gesture.*) Your turn,
Miss Morality. You look somewhat indignant. Or
perhaps (*charmingly, but with mild irony*) it's your so-called
postulates that are troubling you? (*Gaily.*) That's a
sign of advancing age. (*Intimately.*) The Liberal out-
look or the memory of even more antiquated philoso-
phies is of course a burdensome heritage. You must
get rid of it . . . if you feel like it. I'm not demanding,
only advising. After all, we cannot come into conflict
with each other. I respect you and recognise your
rights, rules and indispensability; you, on your part,
will not bother yourself with the fact that within my
own sphere certain changes in interpretation have been
effected. Why not? The cannibal regards it not only
as important and pleasant, but also as deeply moral to
eat his slain enemy; similarly, it's moral considerations
that lead the vegetarian to live on grass. So let everyone be moral in his own way, but don't let's interfere
with each other; do take my advice, Miss Morality.
I'm not persecuting you merely because our views are
different. Please don't preach that we're immoral
merely because our morals are different. (*Menacingly.*)
Can I rely on you?

MORALITY (*old lady dowdily dressed in black, with huge*

diamond twinkling on her bosom ; steps forward uncertainly, in an anxious tone) : I . . . I think so, Herr Fuehrer. *(Backs into her former place.)*

HITLER : Thanks. Why so sad, Reverend Church ? Don't you know that every religion enjoys equality in my Reich ? Your followers are free to make their offerings to you. I've imposed no restriction, no spiritual restriction on you. All I ask is that you should not bother about anything but your own avocation. It isn't worth while, either, believe me. Politics is a disgusting trade, education a bore, culture complicated and uncertain, while as to economics, why, that's filthy. Surely I know what the spirit is, what spirituality is, I, the sworn enemy of Liberal materialism. You'll find me a friend, a supporter and if necessary a defender. I'm a religious man myself. I often call upon God. *(Breaks off in embarrassment, gives a cough, jerks his head round and looks behind him, pulls himself together ; former tone.)* Don't let's be hostile with each other. I'm prepared to enter into a concordat, even to grant you autonomy. But let's be fair. Let's give to God what belongs to God and, er . . . give to me what belongs to me. I know your power, *(somewhat menacing)* and your weaknesses. . . . *(Persuasive.)* Do let's be friends !

THE CHURCH *(stern old priest, in plain black gown ; steps forward, says nothing, but, with a distrustful and uncertain movement, as though he could not help himself, he gives a slight nod, then steps back into the row).*

HITLER *(stares at him for a moment savagely, then in a charming tone)* : Thank you, thank you. *(Lively.)* Well, my dear World Economy. Why that wry expression ? Indigestion ? Chronic crisis ? Or is there anything wrong with the circulation ? Or is it neurasthenia, perhaps ? There's a remedy for everything. For instance, what I want is that production and consumption should balance in accordance with social requirements, as well as in accordance with your interests. That there should be no overproduction and surplus anywhere, but no unemployment and scarcity either. I think we're agreed on that. I want capital to produce a fair interest, and labour a fair wage. I want the world markets to be open to everyone and the sources of raw material to be accessible to all according to their needs. On the other hand, I want nothing to go to waste, either energy or goods. I want money to have its value and to function as an intermediary between the economies of the various nations. Above all, I want it to be sound. Let us regulate the question of international exchanges by agreement. I want everybody to live in plenty . . . with a few quite insignificant exceptions. The question as to who should belong to this minority will settle itself in time, what ? (*Dreamy tone.*) The Golden Age. . . . That's the least I want to achieve. (*Low, familiar.*) I'm prepared to do business. . . .

WORLD ECONOMY (*wry-faced, corpulent old man in lounge suit, with trilby hat in his hand, huge safe key under right arm, huge ledger under left arm; steps forward, bows*): O.K., Adolf Hitler.

HITLER : Thanks. So that's settled. And now— you, my dear. . . . Are you afraid of me ? Come closer, miss.

PEACE (*in its well-known symbolic shape, in a white gown, with drooping wings, barefoot, carrying a faded olive branch; the figure is thin, modest, timid*): I'd like to . . . but I daren't. . . . You've often said such funny things about me. . . .

HITLER (*uproarious laughter*) : Me ? Your best friend ?

You misunderstand the situation entirely, my dear girl. I like you. I want peace in the world. (*Reproving.*) Perhaps the reason for your distrust is that you haven't learned your history properly? We Germans are a peaceful race. We've always been the attacked, not the attackers. Sometimes we even didn't defend ourselves. We never sought war . . . always hated it . . . and anyone who says the contrary (*angry*) is a liar. It was the British who invented the formula, "struggle for existence." There's something in it, though. Life itself is said to be nothing but a struggle. But I always wanted peace, and still do. It was never my fault. They wouldn't believe me, wouldn't understand me, that was how the mistakes were made. (*Bellowing.*) How dare anyone say that I don't want peace, peace within my country, peace in the whole world. My people has been working for peace for a thousand years. (*Charmingly.*) I want peace—almost at any price. I've one or two little demands that must be satisfied—after that your kingdom may come. Do you think I could talk to you like this if I weren't genuinely attracted to you? Don't believe what my enemies the warmongers say. Believe me, instead, my dear. Why don't you answer? Don't you believe me? I want you to, very much. (*In a terrible voice.*) I want peace!

PEACE (*frightened, trembling, with head drawn into shoulders, steps forward; almost inaudibly*): Oh . . . yes, War Lord. (*Resumes place in row.*)

> *Left side is plunged into darkness, while platform remains illuminated.* HITLER *slowly turns to face the audience with a staring look, then, after a moment he veers towards the right, which suddenly lights up, revealing the National Socialist General Staff.*

HITLER (*stares at them, then, pointing*) : Frank ! Prepare the Jew Law. A Jew cannot be a citizen of the Reich, he has no rights, his property is to be confiscated, he must not engage in any trade or profession. The Jew must be eliminated from the life of the nation. I will extirpate the Jew from the world.

FRANK : Jawohl, mein Fuehrer.

HITLER : Streicher ! See to it that the anti-Jewish temper doesn't abate even for an hour. Invent more horrors, more fakes like the *Protocols of the Elders of Zion*, force the tension to bursting point—and let it burst !

STREICHER : Jawohl, mein Fuehrer.

HITLER : Himmler ! Fill the concentration camps. Put in the Jews, put in everyone who's against us even in his secret dreams. Give an example that'll terrify the country and horrify the world. My power can only be consolidated for good by the suffering of others. Guilty or innocent, what does it matter ; we can't afford to be sentimental. Study every trick of the Spanish Inquisition, intensify them a hundredfold, let your imagination soar. You must be everywhere—in the offices, the streets, private homes, in men's very brains, digging up their secret thoughts. . . . You must have an iron fist . . . let the masses tremble. The terrified obey !

HIMMLER : Jawohl, mein Fuehrer.

HITLER : You, Goebbels, drive the people mad. Full steam ahead with the propaganda machine. Feeling and opinion must be with me everywhere ; destroy everything that's against me. The State is the Party, and the Party is me. Smash every human relationship, set child against parent, friend against friend, man against woman. Let everyone distrust everyone else

. . . let everyone have only one faith : me. (*Angrily*.)
To hell with education ! It's poison for the masses and
a dangerous weapon in the hands of the individual.
What the world needs is not civilisation but discipline ;
what I demand is not knowledge but obedience. (*Rage*.)
To hell with morality ! Morality's a drag on determination, it's the superstition of a dead era ! Morality must
be extirpated ! Put National Socialist consciousness in
its place ! Let it penetrate to the very blood of the
German people that they're living for war—that their
ancestors decayed in peace and became great only
through conflict. Perpetual war, war against everything and everyone. The Germans are the master race
and master is he who has the power. The German
must know not how to live, but how to die. Let him
live dangerously. Get at the young, kill their intelli-
gence, teach them strength, violence, hatred—and blind
faith in me. Raise worthy successors to the terrorised,
submissive masses, and raise the elect few to be worthy
successors to me : create a new nobility that knows
how to rule—and how to make the rest of the world
tremble ! Everything and everybody who preaches the
contrary or even imagines the contrary must perish.
Don't tolerate any other spirit than the one fashioned
after my image. Let your voice be heard everywhere
in the world, worm your way in with money, flattery,
irony, threats. Destroy what they believe in or love,
smash their resistance to us. It's a great task for you—
to unlock every door for me.

GOEBBELS : Jawohl, mein Fuehrer.

HITLER : Hess ! . . . Your arm must also reach
wherever there are people in the world and Germans
among them. Every German belongs to me, no matter
where he lives. The laws of their adopted country can

only bind them until they come into conflict with my laws. Don't let them raise in the schools (*contemptuously*) loyal patriots, but loyal National Socialists and Germans, Germans ! Their organisations must not jibber about minority rights or sentimentalise over the old country ; they must keep their eyes and ears open : every German living abroad must be my spy and agent. Let them beware, for the day's approaching when I shall raise up or smite down. Let them stay where they are, eat their way into the body of the foreign nation, enmesh its vital organs, occupy the key positions and await my orders.

HESS : Jawohl, mein Fuehrer.

HITLER : Frick ! Break the power of the priesthood. Confiscate the property of the churches, take the schools out of their hands, choke the word into their gizzards, eject them from the cultural field. Accuse the monks and nuns of currency smuggling, perverted practices ; disgrace them and condemn them. Break up the divine services, close the churches, educate the children to paganism. Send Niemoeller to a concentration camp. We know no distinction between one religion and another : every religion must perish. We must be either religious or German, we cannot be both—and we want to be German and National Socialist.

FRICK : Jawohl, mein Fuehrer.

HITLER : Ribbentrop ! Go and prepare the path for my world power. Make agreements, but don't keep them if my interests demand it so. Disturb the peace of the nations, make them quarrel with each other, incite the strong against the weak—that'll make them weak as well. See that my secret message reaches all the discontented in the other countries, promise them power under my rule if they help me to achieve power.

Break the internal resistance of every country, undermine the morale of the masses, make them believe that
things as they are are bad and that I will bring them
salvation.   Convince the doubting that they will be
serving their country in reality only if they betray it
and sell it to me.   Convince them that they'll be serving
their own interests as well in this way.   Their reward
will be generous if they serve me well.   But I'll have
no welcome for late-comers.   They'd better know that.

RIBBENTROP : Jawohl, mein Fuehrer.

HITLER : Goering ! Build up the strongest army in
the world.   Make tanks like prehistoric monsters, invent the most terrible explosives, make bombs that'll
destroy entire districts, prepare poison gas one breath
of which will kill a city.   I want twice as many warplanes as all the other nations put together.   Organise
parachute divisions, armoured storm battalions, build
thousands of invasion barges, hundreds of warships
and submarines . . . accomplish that which will defeat
the imagination.   Build in the West a belt of fortifi-
cations that'll be stronger than the Alps, build aerodromes, naval ports, barracks, drill centres.   Every
mark—even the money we haven't got—every ounce
of material, every muscle, every nerve, the toil of every
moment must be in the service of this one aim.   Turn
the whole of Germany into one vast military camp—
every man and woman, every boy and girl must learn
to carry arms from infancy.   Produce perambulators
that are armed with machine-guns, and coffins that will
convert the corpses into bacterial bombs.   Think out
and realise a complete autarchy, complete self-suffi-
ciency.   Grow and make everything on German soil,
from the food we eat to the raw material for armaments.
Make this country independent of the rest of the world,

if necessary shut it off hermetically. Make substitutes where you lack the natural product, make artificial petrol for my tanks and 'planes, artificial cloth for uniforms, artificial food, artificial sleep for the exhausted, and artificial blood—No ! The blood must be natural, pure Aryan German blood. Increase and multiply. I want two hundred and fifty million Germans to rule the two and a half milliard people of the world. Build, so that I might later destroy. And destroy so that I might rebuild the world according to my will. Destroy the value of gold, destroy international trade, burn up our connection with world economy. There must remain only one word in the German dictionary : rearmament !

GOERING : Jawohl, mein Fuehrer.

HITLER : And get ready for war. The ancient German way of life is war. For a thousand years we Germans sought conflict, loved a martial existence. In peace you become flaccid, it undermines your will, makes your spirit apathetic. I'm going to fulfil the mission of the German people. My mission. Prepare for war in your waking hours, in your sleep, in your work, in your leisure, in your distractions, with every drop of your blood and every thought of your brain. No mercy, no humanity, no understanding. (*Raving.*) I want war. I want war.

ALL (*with arms raised in salute*) : Jawohl, mein Fuehrer.

Blackout.

CURTAIN.

ACT III

SCENE I

Spring, 1939. *Street in the outskirts of Berlin. The centre of the scene represents the entrance and windows of a baker's shop. The entrance is closed, and so are the shops to the right and left, as the time is early morning. The baker's shop bears the notice :* " *We Open at* 9." *Silence.*

Two Policemen (*come slowly and mutely from the left, stop for an instant to look round, then exeunt right*).

The stage is empty for a few seconds ; it becomes lighter ; sound of tramping feet approaches off, then :

SS Troop (*march stiffly across the stage from right to left*).

Stage is again empty for a few seconds ; distant buzz of motor traffic ; somewhere a clock strikes six.

A Woman (*comes hurrying from left and takes up a position by the entrance of the baker's shop ; she wears a shawl and carries a shopping basket. To herself, low*): Ah, I'm first. I'm lucky this morning. (*Puts basket on the ground.*) Wish it were nine. . . . Must hurry to the butcher . . . opens at eleven this morning . . . perhaps the queue won't be long. . . . Then the grocer. . . . Open all day . . . but has he got anything, that's the question. . . . (*Extracts shopping bag from basket, finds a scrap of paper in it, reads to herself.*) Bread, flour, semolina. A pound of calf's liver, if there isn't any, lung, if there isn't any, tripe, if there isn't any, scraps. Then potatoes, spinach, lettuce, pepper. . . . I want some lamp oil, too. . . . (*Sigh.*) Oh dear. . . .

THE SECOND WOMAN (*comes hurrying from left*):
Hello, Frau Mayer . . . so you're first.

THE FIRST WOMAN: Hello, Frau Schulz. You're
early enough, aren't you. You know, last Friday all
the bread was gone before my turn came, so I made
sure this morning. Don't want to cop it from my
husband again.

THE THIRD WOMAN (*comes from left*): Morning, Frau
Mayer, morning Frau Schulz. (*The other two acknow-
ledge this.*) Cool morning, isn't it. Of course, it's early
yet. You know, I don't really mind, it's much better
to queue up early. Last Saturday afternoon Frau
Huber comes dashing upstairs to me all out of breath.
Hurry up, Frau Kloepke, she sez, there's a queue outside the butcher's at the corner, she sez, he's got some
meat in, I think, she sez, I'm not going to-day because
I haven't got any money, she sez. A good thing you
told me, Frau Huber, I sez, we haven't had any meat
for a month, I sez. Well, so I run along and there was
really a queue in front of the butcher's, two hundred
people at least, but I took my place just the same. I
stood there from half-past twelve till half-past three,
being grilled by the sun, and do you know what I got?
A pound of pig's trotters.

THE SECOND WOMAN: That's something, Frau
Kloepke. Sometimes you don't even get a bit of bone
to give a little strength to your soup.

THE FIRST WOMAN: And sometimes you don't have
a bit of lard or marge left. . . . (*Laugh.*) As to butter,
it's a long time since we had any of that.

THE SECOND WOMAN: But we've got guns, Frau
Mayer.

THE THIRD WOMAN (*looks round anxiously*): Careful,
Frau Schulz! A woman in the queue in front of the

dairy the other day said the same and before she finished the sentence there was a detective, I don't know where he sprung from, but he just took the woman out of that queue and went off with her.

THE SECOND WOMAN : Don't you worry about me, Frau Kloepke. They don't frighten me. I say what I think, even to the detective—and even to Himmler himself, come to that. (*Looks round involuntarily ; more cautiously.*) Those two policemen (*indicating left*) are at least a hundred yards away. (*More loudly.*) Yes, I'll say it right out—the shops are empty and we're always hungry, hungrier than we ever were during the World War. Yet it's peace time now, isn't it ? And who's got their bellies full ?

THE FOURTH WOMAN (*from right*) : Morning, ladies. (*Glances at shop door.*) They open at nine, do they. Gracious, what a long time to wait. Still, so long as we get anything. I want a little white flour. My little Fritz is ten to-morrow and I want to make him a nice apple pie. He loves apple pie, does Fritz, though he hardly remembers the taste of it by now.

THE SECOND WOMAN : As I was saying, Frau Kloepke—who's got their bellies full ? The big shots in the Party ! Yet they don't work fourteen and sixteen hours a day in the factory like my husband.

THE FOURTH WOMAN : Don't talk like that, Frau Schulz ! If anyone hears you we'll all be getting into trouble.

THE FIFTH AND SIXTH WOMAN (*come from left, say good morning, join the queue*).

THE SECOND WOMAN (*carried away by her own impetus*) : I don't care if they cut my head off, I'll have my say just the same. Ten years ago, when Bortke talked my husband into leaving the Socialists and joining the Nazi

Party they all said that the Nazi Party was the place for every decent German working man because the Fuehrer wants to make things good for the German worker, so he won't have to work hard, but get good wages. Well, all I can say is this, that they took the factory away from the Jew who owned it. . . . I don't care about that, it's not my business . . . but it is my business that my Karl has got to work six or eight hours more than before and they pay him less than the Jew did, and it wouldn't make no difference if they paid him more because I can't buy nothing with the money (*hissing contempt*) unless it's pig's trotters.

THE FIFTH WOMAN : My husband gets five marks a week stopped out of his wages for the people's car. We've had a hundred and seventy-five marks stopped already, and where's the people's car? In the book where they put down the instalments and nowhere else. We don't want it, neither, but when they told my husband that we must pay the money because the Fuehrer wants every working man to have a people's car we said to ourselves, well, if we must, we must, it'll do for our Heinrich, he's crazy on cars. Just think of it, he's only sixteen and they've taught him at school to pick a machine-gun to pieces and put it together again, just like a soldier. But he sez he doesn't want to be a foot soldier, but a flier. (*Uncertainly.*) He sez they'll teach him to jump out of the aeroplane with a kind of umbrella. It makes me shiver to think of it. But Heinrich's quite crazy on it, he sez every German boy must learn to do it because there's going to be a war with Russia and France.

THE SIXTH WOMAN (*sagely*) : We're going to have a war all right. As I keep saying to my Max, we're Germans all right, but we're working people, so why

do the big shots in the Party keep running down the
foreign working people and say they're Socialists and
Communists and, er . . . plutocrats.

THE FIRST WOMAN : Not plutocrats—democrats,
Social Democrats. Plutocrats are something else. That
means the rich . . . I think.

THE SECOND WOMAN (*makes a wry face*) : That's all
the better, then. You know, last year I used to oblige
at a family called Heinz. The man's a big Party man
and an SA commander. They live in Grunewald, in a
big villa, they'd only just bought it, and they've about
fifteen rooms, though Herr Heinz is quite young, and
they have three motor-cars and the poshest furniture
you ever saw. They had a maid who used to be in
service with some Jews round there and she sez that
even the Jews didn't show off like the Heinzes, and
Goering used to call on them, and the year before last
he sent the woman a tea-set of pure gold for a Christmas
box. So now I know who are the plutocrats.

THE SEVENTH, EIGHTH, NINTH AND TENTH WOMAN
(*arrive, join the queue*).

THE FOURTH WOMAN : Take up your places, or else
people what come later'll get in front of you.

THE TENTH WOMAN : Gracious, there are many of
us already and I'm having an extra washing day because
my boy's going camping with the Hitler Youth on
Thursday and I must give him some clean linen.

THE SEVENTH WOMAN : My boy went camping
last week, and him with a cough and a temperature,
too ; but he wouldn't listen to me, he said it'd be a disgrace if he didn't go and he'd run away if I didn't let
him. What a life !

THE EIGHTH WOMAN : Do you know what happened to my boy ? He's eleven, my Joseph is, and the

114

other day they marched out and the group leader, a nasty brat of fourteen, suddenly dashes up to my Joseph and shouts you clumsy lout, is that the way to march? and he kicks him on the shin, so the poor dear fell over and he could hardly limp home. (*Gesture.*) His leg got swollen as big as this, and he had to stay in bed for a week. I wanted to go to the school and complain, but my boy wouldn't let me, he said the group leader was right, because if a boy didn't do things right he had to be disciplined. What do you say to that! What's going to become of children like that, I wonder—one of them a beastly hooligan and the other thinks it's right for him to be kicked. Is this what German boys ought to be like?

THE NINTH WOMAN: You better be careful with your tongue, Frau Weber.

> *Some ten or fifteen more women arrive in rapid succession; the flow continues during the rest of the scene. The new arrivals exchange greetings with the others, join in general conversation; queue grows to enormous length.*

A WOMAN IN BLACK SHAWL (*arrives, leading thin, nervy little boy of ten by the hand*): Morning. I'm late.

THE EIGHTH WOMAN: Never mind, you'll get your turn just the same.

THE WOMAN IN BLACK SHAWL: If there's anything to have my turn for. (*To* BOY.) Don't fidget, Hansi.

THE BOY: Must I stay here, Mum?

THE WOMAN IN BLACK SHAWL: There's nowhere you can go, Hansi, there's no school, and I may have to stand here for hours and you can't be alone at home.

THE BOY: Why not? All the other boys can. Why didn't you let me go camping, then? All the other boys've gone, and you went and begged them to let me off.

THE WOMAN IN BLACK SHAWL: You know your father may be back this week. I wanted him to find you at home. You know very well that's why I got you excused.

THE FIRST WOMAN (*low*): Is this the Frau Muller whose husband's in the concentration camp?

THE SECOND WOMAN (*ditto*): Yes.

THE THIRD WOMAN (*ditto*): He's in Dachau?

THE SECOND WOMAN: Yes.

THE THIRD WOMAN: Why did they send him there?

THE SECOND WOMAN (*wave of the hand*): God knows.

AN OLD JEWESS (*comes uncertainly from right with shopping-bag on her arm; she shuffles past the queue, returns, shuffles back as far as its centre, stops a few paces from queue and looks at it*).

THE FIFTH WOMAN: What're you stopping for? You know they don't serve Jews.

THE OLD JEWESS: I know. They don't serve Jews. (*Mumbling to herself.*) The baker, the butcher, the grocer, the dairy . . . they've got nothing for the Jews. Nothing for the Jews. (*Shuffles out left.*)

THE BOY (*steps out of queue, shouting after her*): Dirty Jewess! Jewish sow!

THE WOMEN (*look at the boy, are silent*).

THE WOMAN IN BLACK SHAWL (*seizes him by the arm*): Hans!

THE EIGHTH WOMAN: I wouldn't mind them serving the Jews—if only there was anything to serve them with.

THE NINTH WOMAN: Better not say it aloud, Frau Rempolt.

THE SECOND WOMAN: Why shouldn't she, if she feels like it?

THE THIRD WOMAN: You're allowed to talk, aren't you?

THE NINTH WOMAN : Of course you aren't. You aren't even allowed to think. Better keep quiet. You'll only get yourself into trouble.

THE WOMAN IN BLACK SHAWL : That's right. My husband told the truth, just spoke his mind, and he's had to suffer for it. He said that we working people, we the German people didn't want *this*, not this. (*Darkly.*) They took him six months ago. He's in Dachau. A young lawyer friend of ours, son of a working man, has been trying to do something for him. He said last week that he'd managed with a lot of trouble to get them to let him out. He may be back home in a few days. (*Gloomily.*) All the same, it's hard for honest folk not to think and to keep on keeping quiet.

A cold silence pervades the queue for a moment.

THE EIGHTH WOMAN (*quietly*) : Well . . . it's a hard life, for sure.

THE SEVENTH WOMAN : Isn't it, just. You hear all sorts of things. (*Uncertainly.*) You know, we're friendly with a neighbour, name of Gruber. He's foreman at the dyeworks, but just now they're not making dyes but some kind of gun-powder . . . explosives. (*Warming to it.*) Well, they've got a daughter, Grete, she'll be sixteen next autumn. Well, the other evening they were sitting at supper and Grete was taken ill, she went pale and began to tremble and heave, and then she fainted. Well, Frau Gruber kept blaming herself for having bought horse sausage for supper, but Grete came to herself again and she said there was nothing the matter with her. But guess what happened. Two days later Grete was taken ill again, with her head swimming, and being sick and fainting. What'd you think of it ?

THE NINTH WOMAN (*excited*) : Well ?

THE FOURTH WOMAN : You don't mean——

THE SEVENTH WOMAN : I certainly do. Yes, that was it. She was pregnant. Well, her mother gives a scream, her father makes to give her a good lacing, and do you know what the girl did ? She turned on her own parents and said to leave her alone, she knows what she's doing and she's proud of it because it's the duty of every German girl to have lots of children, and she doesn't want the man who got her into trouble to marry her . . . it was an SA man from the next block, so I heard. . . . Well, she sez, don't you keep on at me, the time's past when parents could order their children about. But that isn't all. (*Becomes agitated.*) When poor Frau Gruber collected herself like, she sez to Grete, she sez, we must do something, she sez, her father and grandfather and all the rest of her family were respectable working men, and so was Gruber's family, and she couldn't bear the disgrace and they must do something, you know. . . . (*Gesture.*) Then Grete started to scream and carry on something awful. She said it's no disgrace for a German girl to have a baby, it's an honour, she said, and the baby belongs to the German people and a lot more rubbish, and then she said if her parents tried to do anything about it she'd run along and give them up. Her own parents !

SEVERAL WOMEN : Isn't it awful ! Heartless hussy ! A young child like that ! She'd have sent her own parents to Dachau ! Would you have believed it !

THE WOMAN IN BLACK SHAWL : That's because they've taken our children away from us. Because they've taught them to love no one, respect no one, except (*after looking round*) him, Hitler.

THE SIXTH WOMAN : Careful, Frau Muller !

THE EIGHTH WOMAN : Well, she's perfectly right.

THE WOMAN IN BLACK SHAWL : Because our children do nothing but march and fight. Because they're playing at war instead of getting educated. Because they're not raising them to be people, but wild beasts.

THE SECOND WOMAN : Frau Muller, I'm afraid you're going a bit too far.

THE FIRST WOMAN : She's perfectly right, I say. (*Suddenly reckless.*) It's true—they're teaching our children to be wild beasts. You listen to this. I've a little nephew, Herbert's his name and he's now nine. When he was six his parents had to let him join the Hitler Cubs. They gave him a little uniform and a little dagger—a real dagger, mind you. Well, the other afternoon Herbert comes home from drill dog tired and asks for some bread and jam. My sister-in-law says, " No, Herbert, you can't have any now, we're having supper directly and I don't want you to spoil your appetite." So Herbert says, " You wait, Mummy, I'll tell the group leader the way you treat me, but I'm not going to beg you for a bit of bread and jam, I'll go and get what I want." Well, my sister-in-law has a quick temper and she gave Herbert a tiny slap on the face—a real mother can't hit her own child really hard. And do you know what the boy did ? (*Hysterical agitation.*) He drew his dagger and went for his mother ! My sister-in-law caught his hand just in time, but she cut herself badly and her hand was bandaged for a time. Well, my brother-in-law went to the Party and told them what happened and he asked to whom he should go to get this sort of thing stopped because it was intolerable. What do you think they told him ? That he'd better hold his tongue and say nothing about the matter because it shows that they're bringing up the boy in the wrong way and he might be taken away from them. . . . You'd think he meant they weren't strict enough with the boy, wouldn't you? Well, you'd be wrong. The man at the Party said: "You fool, what've you got to complain about, you ought to be glad to have such a boy, such a proud German and such a good Nazi. . . ." And he said to be careful or else they'd watch his behaviour in future—my brother-in-law's behaviour, if you please! (*Sweeping gesture.*) Well, that's how things are. (*Suddenly scared, shrinks within herself.*) I wish it were nine o'clock already and they'd open the blessed shop.

THE WOMAN IN BLACK SHAWL: Yes, we've got *that*, but not enough to eat. The bread, the meat, the potatoes and all the rest is only for those who (*gesture*) are up there, speechifying and riding in motor-cars and wearing posh uniforms and living in magnificent palaces. Yes. Now we know, we poor people, what the Nazi heaven's like.

THE BOY (*slinks away unobserved to right*).

THE THIRD WOMAN: But we've got Strength through Joy, we have. Do you know where my brother's been? In America. He's a great Nazi, so they took him to New York for three weeks along with about a hundred and twenty aircraft workers.

THE FIRST WOMAN: La-la, he must've seen a lot of fine things.

THE THIRD WOMAN: La-la . . . he didn't see anything at all. They took them by car from the ship straight to their lodgings, somewhere in the outskirts it was, in a German colony. Then they took them by car from one German settlement to another and to all sorts of German camps, because it was some sort of

120

Nazi Week, and so my brother saw the German men's camp and the German women's camp and the German boys' camp and the German girls' camp and he marched and heiled a lot—and that was all.

THE FIFTH WOMAN: Surely, they must've seen something—the big buildings at least.

THE THIRD WOMAN: Well, perhaps they couldn't hide those from them. But the guides never left them for a minute, in case they took a few steps on their own. Or in case they saw what things are like out there. There were German meetings, and more German meetings, and a march-past before some German-American Fuehrer, not much more. Of course, my brother wasn't very pleased. My husband said why don't we go to Italy with the Strength through Joy, but I'll have none of it, I won't.

THE FOURTH WOMAN: Who the devil wants to go to Italy? I'd rather have enough to wear. Last winter I wanted to buy a pair of winter shoes. There weren't any. A winter coat for my daughter. There wasn't any. A warm jerkin for my husband. There wasn't any. Strength through Joy, indeed! We'd get the strength all right from enough to eat and enough to wear. But *we* are not entitled to that. The right to an easy life belongs to . . . to other people.

THE FIRST WOMAN: I wonder if I'll get to the butcher this morning.

THE SECOND WOMAN: It goes on like this all through the week.

THE SEVENTH WOMAN: What about Sunday? My husband gets up at six on week-days to be at the works by seven, but on Sunday he's got to get up at four because he's got to go marching at five. You see, he's an honorary group leader in the SA and there's drill on Sundays.

THE FOURTH WOMAN : My husband's in another sort of trouble. He's been working on agricultural machinery for twenty-four years and now, since February of last year his works've been making armaments and he hasn't been able to get the hang of it yet. A harvester and a machine-gun are two different things.

THE SIXTH WOMAN : My younger sister is making rifle bullets instead of cigarette boxes.

THE WOMAN IN BLACK SHAWL : That's what they're all making, arms and munitions. It's wanted for the war. Because there's going to be one. My elder brother fought for four years in the World War and got wounded three times, and when he came home in nineteen-eighteen he said, well, what was the use of killing all those millions of people ? But *they* . . . they say the killing must start all over again. Not so as to make our lot better, but so that *they* can have more. They don't say so in the Party, but it's true just the same.

THE THIRD WOMAN : Frau Muller, one of these days you'll get into serious trouble. They may send you to join your husband in Dachau.

THE WOMAN IN BLACK SHAWL : What do I care ! It's all the same to me. Go on, Frau Kloepke, denounce me.

THE THIRD WOMAN (*offended*) : Who do you think I am !

THE NINTH WOMAN : She's only warning you for your own sake.

THE EIGHTH WOMAN : We give you up ? That's an insult, Frau Muller. You know very well that we all know——— (*Breaks off.*)

Two POLICEMEN *and a* DETECTIVE *have appeared from right. Behind them, with a sidling gait, comes the* BOY. *Two* POLICEMEN *and a* DETECTIVE *slowly walk along the queue, then return and stop facing the middle of the queue, with backs to the audience. The* BOY *is now standing by the wall on the right, at the end of the queue.*

THE DETECTIVE (*stands gazing at the women, then suddenly raises his right arm and points at the* WOMAN IN THE BLACK SHAWL) : Come here. You.

THE WOMAN IN BLACK SHAWL : Me ?

THE DETECTIVE : Yes, you. You're Frau Muller, aren't you ?

THE WOMAN IN BLACK SHAWL : Yes, Frau Anton Muller. (*Suddenly.*) Is it a message from home . . . my husband . . . has he arrived ?

THE DETECTIVE (*slowly, in measured tones*) : Frau Anton Muller. . . . (*Frigidly.*) You wanted to let a Jewess join the queue ?

THE WOMAN IN BLACK SHAWL (*amazed*) : Me ? I never saw . . . (*uncertainly*) I mean I did see her, but I didn't speak to her.

SEVERAL WOMEN (*together*) : She didn't want to let her come here. We none of us wanted to do that. The Jewess didn't even try to join us, she went away of her own accord.

THE DETECTIVE (*roughly*) : You shut up. I didn't ask you. (*To* WOMAN IN BLACK SHAWL.) You said that the bread, the meat, the potatoes are for those who sit in motor-cars and wear posh uniforms ?

THE WOMAN IN BLACK SHAWL (*aghast*) : Me . . . I said that . . . (*Stops.*)

THE DETECTIVE : You said that now we know what the Nazi heaven's like ?

THE WOMAN IN BLACK SHAWL (*stammering*) : I . . . I only said that . . . (*Stops.*)

THE DETECTIVE (*looks round, beckons to the* BOY) : Come here, boy.

THE BOY (*sidles up*).

WOMEN (*low buzz among them*).

THE DETECTIVE : Was it your mother who told that Jewess to queue up ?

THE BOY (*low*) : Yes, sir.

THE WOMAN IN BLACK SHAWL : It's not true ! Hans, you mustn't lie.

THE DETECTIVE : Was it your mother who said she knew what the Nazi heaven was like and who got the bread and the meat.

THE BOY (*low*) : Yes, sir.

THE WOMAN IN BLACK SHAWL (*almost fainting with fright*) : I . . . I only meant . . . I . . .

THE DETECTIVE (*interrupting*) : You see, Frau Muller. . . . You better explain what you meant at the station. (*Motions to* POLICEMEN.) Come along.

THE POLICEMEN (*step on each side of the woman*).

THE WOMAN IN BLACK SHAWL (*low scream*) : I can't go . . . I can't . . . I'm expecting my husband back. . . . I can't leave my boy by himself.

THE DETECTIVE : Come along quietly. . . . We don't want to attract a crowd.

THE POLICEMAN (*takes her by the arm, low*) : Come along now. (*Gently propels her forward.*)

THE WOMAN IN BLACK SHAWL (*between the two* POLICEMEN, *stumbles forward, then pulls herself together, raises her head*) : All right, then, take me ! Lock me up ! Kill me ! It'll be better than to live like this. (*Exeunt.*)

THE DETECTIVE : Well, boy. We'll follow them. (*Exeunt.*)

The whole queue stands petrified. Dead silence. This is broken by a sudden rattling noise. Door of baker's shop opens.

THE BAKER (*appears in door*) : Sorry, ladies, the goods haven't arrived after all, we've nothing to sell.

Silence.

THE BAKER : I'm very sorry. . . . Better go home. Try again to-morrow.

THE FIRST WOMAN : But . . . if there's no bread, then at least a little flour or something. . . .

THE SECOND WOMAN : We've been standing here since six o'clock. . . .

THE BAKER (*impatient*) : Sorry, ladies, there's nothing at all this morning, neither bread nor anything else. Perhaps to-morrow.

THE THIRD WOMAN : We'll come again to-morrow and stand again for hours and get nothing.

Low murmur among the crowd of women.

THE BAKER (*irritably*) : You talk as if it were my fault. Go away. It's forbidden to collect in front of a shop when there's no opportunity to buy. If you don't disperse at once I'll have to call a policeman. Go away. Heil Hitler !

Silence, the women make no move.

THE BAKER (*steps back, closes door from the inside, removes card, draws curtain*).

THE FOURTH WOMAN : So that's how it is. (*Brief silence.*) Well, good-bye, ladies.

OTHERS (*low*) : Good-bye.

They disperse silently. The stage is empty for a moment. The sun is up.

QUICK CURTAIN.

SCENE II

Early summer, 1939. *Frontier post. Downstage right, a*
FRONTIER GUARD *in grey coat reaching to the ground*
and grey cap. He keeps one hand on a lengthy pole
bearing a flag combined from the flags and emblems of
many nations. Some three paces from him, towards left
centre, a desk, at which sits the IMMIGRATION OFFICER
in long grey overcoat. Running upstage as far as extreme
left at the back is a barrier. The whole is set in a black
circular backcloth. Vivid light on post itself, rest of
the stage is in darkness. At extreme upstage left, in
the half-light, we sense the waiting crowd.

At the rise of the curtain there is an instant's
silence, then :

THE OFFICER (*speaking towards left*): Next, please.
(*Aged couple come forward.*)   Your passports, please.

AN OLD MAN (*places two passports on desk*).

THE OFFICER : You belong together ?

THE OLD MAN : Yes, sir.   She's my wife.

THE OFFICER (*examining passports*) : Yes.   You're
Albert Ehrbahr.

THE OLD MAN : Yes.

THE OFFICER : Age ?

THE OLD MAN : Seventy-two.

THE OFFICER : You're a doctor ?

THE OLD MAN : Yes.   I'm a University professor
. . . I mean was.

THE OFFICER : You come from Vienna ?

THE OLD MAN : Vienna . . . that's where they
drove us out from.

THE OFFICER : You're Jewish ?

THE OLD MAN (*low*): Half Jewish.   I was born a
Roman Catholic.   My mother came from an old Aus-

trian military family. My father was a converted Jew.
He was a doctor, too, as were my father and his father.

THE OFFICER : Have you any money ?

THE OLD MAN : Ten marks each . . . twenty
marks altogether.

THE OFFICER : Have you any property ?

THE OLD MAN : They took it away.

THE OFFICER : How are you going to live in this
country ?

THE OLD MAN (*very low, embarrassed*) : I have a
friend here. He was my pupil, then for a long time
my collaborator in research. Twenty years ago we
shared the Nobel Prize for Medicine. He'll help me.
And I've hopes that I'll be invited to one of the
Universities in this country.

THE OFFICER : Otherwise . . . you'll have to have
a permit to work. What'll you do if you don't get it ?

THE OLD MAN (*simply*) : I don't know. And frankly
. . . I don't care very much. We don't expect much
from life.

THE OLD WOMAN (*timidly*) : We'd two sons. One
committed suicide, the other was murdered at Dachau.

THE OLD MAN : We shouldn't have wanted to go
on living, but our religion forbids suicide. We
shouldn't even have left Vienna if they hadn't forced us.

THE OFFICER (*clears his throat ; brief silence ; he
hands back passports, waving them towards opening in the
backcloth*) : Very well.

THE OLD MAN : Thank you. (*Exit with* OLD
WOMAN.)

THE OFFICER : Next, please.

 A MAN, *a* WOMAN *and three* CHILDREN *come to
 desk.*

THE OFFICER : You belong together ?

THE MAN: Yes, sir. (*Puts passports on table.*)

THE OFFICER: You're Carl Redlich, business man. What business?

THE MAN: I had a shoe shop in Cologne.

THE WOMAN: They pillaged it last November, during the pogrom. They smashed up the fittings, threw our goods into the street, then they carried them away—the thieves. They picked out what they wanted in the street. This is too small for me.—This is too big for me.—I want a pair of ladies' patent leather shoes.—I want this, I want that——

THE MAN (*pacifying her*): My dear——

THE OFFICER: You're Jewish?

THE MAN: Yes, sir.

THE WOMAN: They set fire to our synagogues— the heathens. When the mob came—you know, sir, there were SA men among them in civilian clothes—I recognised one—he lived in the same house as us. . . . So when they came to destroy and steal the police stood by, grinning. My husband was in the door of the shop trying to pull down the shutters, but he was attacked by ten of them——

THE MAN (*embarrassed*): But, darling, the gentleman's not interested——

THE WOMAN: I want him to know about it!

THE OFFICER: Any money?

THE MAN: We've got ten marks each—fifty marks.

THE OFFICER: Any property?

THE MAN (*waves his hand*).

THE WOMAN: But we had plenty. They stole everything. They wouldn't allow the insurance company to pay for the damage. Because a crazy boy shot a diplomat in Paris they took away nearly all we had. As if they hadn't committed murder. What was their punishment ? (*At one breath.*) They robbed us of what little we had left when we came out, they charged us emigration tax and we had to pay separately for every document, and we always had to slip them something in secret, ten marks here, a hundred marks there, otherwise we'd still be there. We're sorry for what we've lost, no, we gave the money gladly for the sake of the children——

THE MAN : Really, my dear——

THE OFFICER : How are you going to live in this country ? What are you going to do ?

THE MAN : My younger brother's been living here for twenty years. He's naturalised. He's got a cardboard box factory. It was he who got us out. He got me a permit to work. I'll work in his factory (*low*) as a packer.

THE OFFICER (*hands back passports*) : Very well. (*The group passes on.*) Next, please.

A LADY IN FUR CAP (*comes to desk, puts passport on desk*).

THE OFFICER (*examining it*) : You're Caroline Kuenstler ?

THE LADY : Yes.

THE OFFICER : Age forty-five. Occupation ?

THE LADY : I was art mistress in Dresden.

THE OFFICER : Are you alone ? A widow ?

THE LADY : No—divorced. (*Low.*) I'm Jewish, my husband Aryan. I didn't want to ruin his career, I agreed to be divorced. (*Brief pause.*) In any case, the law entitled him to divorce me.

THE OFFICER : Any children ?

THE LADY : A boy of sixteen and a girl of fifteen. They've been sent to another country by an organisation. They hate me because I'm Jewish. For the last six years—since they were little—that's what they heard at school from the other children—to hate the Jews. The poor dears couldn't forgive me having brought them into the world . . . having made them into half-Jews. (*Low.*) They had to suffer on account of me. (*Different tone.*) My husband . . . he's not a bad man . . . but he'd have lost his post if we'd stayed together.

THE OFFICER (*clears his throat*) : Any money ?

THE LADY : Ten marks. All I have in the world.

THE OFFICER : How are you going to live in this country ?

THE LADY (*quickly produces some papers*) : I've got a permit to work. I've got a job to go to. (*Low.*) As a domestic servant. I used to keep a cook and a maid myself. I'm rather afraid . . . but I'll do my best. (*Lamely.*) People are very kind in this country.

THE OFFICER (*casually*) : Yes. Here you are, madam. (*Hands back passport ; gesture towards crowd.*) Next.

THE LADY : Thank you. (*Exits right.*)

A WORKMAN (*comes to desk*).

THE OFFICER : Your passport, please.

THE WORKMAN : Haven't got one.

THE OFFICER : A Nansen passport ? A white paper ?

THE WORKMAN : No, nothing.

THE OFFICER : Then how did you get here ?

THE WORKMAN : I come from Hamburg. My name is Friedrich Stark. Couldn't bear it, sir. No decent man could. So I hid in a ship, down in the hold, and when the ship was nearing the coast I jumped in the sea and swam ashore.

THE OFFICER : That's a punishable offence, you know.

THE WORKMAN : I know, sir. Will they lock me

up? All right. (*Louder.*) But I'm not going back. I'm not a Jew, but I've had enough of the bandits.

THE OFFICER (*uncertainly*): And supposing you're allowed to stay in this country, how are you going to live?

THE WORKMAN (*raises his fist, puts it on the desk*): I can swing a hammer . . . and if necessary I can handle a rifle.

THE OFFICER: Very well, you may go.

THE WORKMAN (*exit right*).

THE OFFICER: Next.

A TALL MAN *and an elegant* BLONDE *come to desk.*

THE OFFICER: You're together?

THE TALL MAN (*clears his throat*): Er . . . yes. We're engaged.

THE BLONDE: And we were unable to marry. (*Vehemently.*) They drove him out, so I'm not going to stay either. My father was a general, he commanded an army corps during the World War. If this is what it was all for, then I don't want them. I've been living with my fiancé for years and I want to stay with him. In this country we can get married. (*Clings to companion's arm.*)

THE OFFICER (*casually*): Your passports, please. (*Examines.*) You're Rolf Reich of Berlin, industrialist?

THE TALL MAN: I was an industrialist. I'm an inventor.

THE OFFICER: Any money?

THE BLONDE: We had twenty marks, twice ten, but we spent it on our breakfast.

THE OFFICER (*smiles to himself*): Any property?

THE TALL MAN: I had a fortune worth millions. They stole it from me. They took my factories, stole my inventions. (*Brief pause.*) Those that were already patented and public. But not (*points at his forehead*) those that I've got here. (*Brief pause.*) Ten years ago they offered me three million marks from this country for an invention. I haven't carried it out yet, but now I can do so. Perhaps they can still use it.

THE OFFICER (*hands back passports*): Very well.

THE TALL MAN: Thanks. (*Exit with* BLONDE.)

THE OFFICER: Next.

Little BOY *and* GIRL *timidly come to desk.*

THE OFFICER (*looks up*): Where are your parents, children? (*Towards the presumed crowd.*) Who do these two children belong to? Come forward, please.

THE BOY (*aged nine*): We're alone, sir.

THE GIRL (*seven*): I'm afraid.

THE OFFICER: Don't be afraid, dear. (*To* BOY.) You're alone? Where's your father and mother?

THE BOY: At home. They didn't come.

THE GIRL: Because Daddy didn't have any money.

THE BOY: So he sent us alone.

THE GIRL: Mummy made cakes to bring with us. I had a dolly as well, but just before the train started a gentleman took it away.

THE OFFICER (*mute, embarrassed, sits gazing at them*).

THE BOY: Daddy said . . . (*as though reciting what he does not understand*) that we must go away because we must be saved. . . .

THE GIRL: I didn't want to leave Daddy and Mummy. (*Sudden.*) I had six dollies and a kitchen and a new baby and a pram and a big doggy with real hair. . . . (*Bursts into tears.*)

THE OFFICER (*badly embarrassed*): Don't cry, little girl.

THE BOY: Daddy said he and Mummy'd come after

us when they had the money, and he said when we grew up we'd go back to them, and he said we must behave, and they're always thinking of us and the Lord will look after us. (*His voice almost breaks, but he pulls himself together and goes on normally.*) Daddy said we must give you these (*takes papers from a little bag*) and ask you to show us where we get on the train.

THE OFFICER: On the train. . . . (*Brief pause.*) And . . . what're you going to do in this country? (*Sudden.*) Where are you going to?

THE GIRL (*cries in a thin voice*).

THE BOY: There are some kind people waiting for us at a station.

THE OFFICER: All right, children. You go along that way. (*Points.*)

THE BOY (*takes* GIRL *by the hand*): Why do you always cry. Come along. (*Exeunt right.*)

THE OFFICER (*after a brief pause*): Next, please.

A MAN IN GREY (*comes to desk, deposits passport and large sheaf of papers*).

THE OFFICER (*surprised*): What's this?

THE MAN IN GREY: My passport and papers—birth certificate, inoculation, health, conduct, means, political, marriage and tax certificates and other personal documents—exit permit, immigration permit, invitations, contracts, promises and vouchers. Residential permits and registration papers. School certificates, references, military and civil decoration awards, University degrees, letters of appreciation from clients, covering notes for some of my visas—the visas are in the passport. (*Indicating papers on desk.*) My past. Presumably also my future.

THE OFFICER: Really, sir——

THE MAN IN GREY: It's all there—all that the

State, the administration and humanity demand and provide. For some of them I studied and worked for years ; for others I stood for hours in long queues day after day outside offices and consulates—separately for each one ; I trembled through sleepless nights in case they refused me this or that paper. There are some that were thrown at me by benevolent foreigners from pity, and there are some that I obtained by bribery from the Nazis. My head's buzzing with the addresses of offices and the names of officials. (*Low.*) That was my chief occupation for the past two years.

THE OFFICER (*somewhat perplexed*): Your passport——

THE MAN IN GREY (*urgently*): It's valid for a good few years yet, though I can't return to my native land with it. There's my name, on the first page. But I think my name doesn't matter. For the past few years I've been more of a cipher—several ciphers, in registers, on queue cards and vouchers. Or they called me " The Refugee " or " The Alien." (*Obligingly, as one who knows all the questions.*) I'm Jewish, sir. . . . My age . . . I've aged a lot lately. . . . Occupation. . . . I had one, I had a career, a successful career, but I have none now. I played my role in my country's intellectual and economic life—a not inconsiderable role. They pushed me out of it. What I'd built up they destroyed or stole from me. I had a fortune, at least a few things I loved ; they were taken from me. Money : the ten marks. I come from Greater Germany, from the Third Reich. Why I left ? Not because of the misery—you can get used to that. But you can't get used to the prison atmosphere. In any case, I was driven out. How I'm going to live in this country ? I don't know. For the present I'd be happiest if I could sit down in a park in the sunshine, on a beach from which they wouldn't chase me away.

THE OFFICER : Yes, yes. . . . But all this is rather uncertain——

THE MAN IN GREY (*sternly*) : Entirely uncertain. But that doesn't matter. Sooner or later you in this country will also realise that the age of certainties is past. It's not our fault, nor yours. But let's reckon with the fact. All we can do is to put up with the uncertainty. (*Indicating the presumed crowd.*) Both I and they. For I'm only one of the crowd, one individual who's got this far. The others, millions of them, are still on the way or preparing for it. We're all coming out of the darkness where we can't bear it any longer. We can't bear the humiliation, the jackboot on our faces, the triumphant guffaw of the barbarians. We're coming from our decayed homes, our broken careers, leaving our all, together with the memory of our pasts and our lifework. We're coming from our disrupted families, we're coming out of our loneliness, our defencelessness. We're coming at the cost of great privations, inhuman sacrifices, sometimes at the cost of petty swindling. We lost all we had, were made to abandon all we loved : the house where we were born, the town where we grew up, the sky, the landscape, the atmosphere in which we became conscious that we belonged somewhere, the cemeteries that hold the bones of our ancestors. All that belongs to the past. We're bringing our bare lives with us. (*Confidentially.*) A mass-produced article, not very valuable—it used to be duty free. We're coming from our fatherland, from Hitler's Empire, and we'll be coming from everywhere where Nazi cunning slithers in, where Nazi violence crashes in, where the crooked cross or one of its variants becomes master. We're coming in an endless procession from the four corners of the earth. We're coming—with official permits or smuggling ourselves through forests and over frontiers, swimming across rivers and trudging over endless roads through the night. We're coming and we don't know how we're going to live, what we're going to do in this country. But don't worry about us . . . and we have a great trust in humanity. The legal expert'll become an errand boy at the grocer's, the doctor'll plant potatoes, the artist'll become a valet, the professor'll sell silk stockings, and the banker may beg his bread from door to door. Anyhow, the majority'll be doing something else than before, something else than what they have talent for, and many will live on charity. Oh, we know we'll have to suffer many indignities, perhaps humiliations, we'll meet with little sympathy and a lot of indifference, perhaps also with some aversion because we're aliens. (*Low.*) The bread will taste different, the air will smell different—it'll all be alien to us. But we don't mind even if all we get is a doss and a crust, because . . . (*gesture*) we want to breathe, freely and deeply . . . because we don't want to start with mortal terror whenever the front door bell rings, we don't want to pale whenever a strange car stops in front of the house, we don't want to have to look round anxiously after every whispered word, we don't want to hang our heads and lower our gaze in the presence of any little runt. We're coming because the cup's at last full, the cup of suffering that nature's fashioned for man. We're coming to save our lives. We're coming because our bodies and souls are long past the limit where they can bear all this abomination, infamy, shame and corruption. (*Gesture.*) Some of you people might

136

say : " That's too bad to be true. Aren't you exaggerating a bit ? " The question wouldn't surprise me. I know you people are not blessed with a vivid imagination. It can't quite grasp what you haven't experienced yourselves, so you don't quite believe it. Besides, you are somewhat distrustful with us. (*Quietly.*) That's difficult for us to bear; that's bad. It's terrible! Because that's how the trouble started everywhere—that they could not imagine what we were telling them and so they wouldn't believe us. " Surely, this is an exaggeration. . . ." (*Vehemently.*) We were *there* and we *know*. We know what they have done, what they want, the Nazi barbarians. And we know what's going to happen where they pooh-pooh what we're saying. We come in an endless procession from all directions ; we come with our ten marks and tattered lives ; we come with our knowledge, energy and will to save ourselves and build for you ; we come and if necessary we face starvation and suffering for the sake of freedom and human dignity—because here, at last, we can hope. . . . We come and our only luggage is our past which was happy, and the memory which is immortal. . . . We come—we, the writing on the wall ; we come, a million grains of dust driven by the wind that precedes the storm, to bring tidings and warn you : Beware! (*Quietly.*) Can I go?

THE OFFICER (*reflects, then*) : Very well.

THE MAN IN GREY : Thanks. (*Exit right.*)

THE OFFICER (*motions towards left*) : Next, please.

The lighted part of the stage gradually darkens. As the curtain slowly descends the crowd from left streams towards the gate in the barrier—they are a moving, milling shadow. We hear the OFFICER's *voice :* " Very well, you may go. . . . Next, please. . . . You may go."

137

SCENE III

Last day of August, 1939. Early evening. HITLER'S *office in the new Chancellery in Berlin. Left, large desk. Back, two large windows, with the German Eagle and the Swastika between them. Right, large double door. Small table in front of desk, also five deep arm-chairs. Windows are curtained. The chandelier is on.*

HITLER (*is sitting at desk with elbows on it and folded hands in front of his face ; he is staring in front of him*).

> *Door quietly opens ; enter, cautiously, the* ADJU-TANT, *a tall young man in Party uniform.*

THE ADJUTANT (*stops six paces from desk, raises arm*) : Heil, mein Fuehrer. The Ambassador has arrived. Shall he wait ?

HITLER (*continues to stare, as though he had not heard, then gives a start*) : No. Show him in.

THE ADJUTANT (*salutes with his arm, exit*).

> *Brief pause. Silence.* HITLER *still sits rigidly. Door opens.*

THE ADJUTANT (*re-enters, stands aside*) : His Excellency the Western Ambassador.

THE AMBASSADOR (*enters ; he is tall, lean, grey-haired ; he wears a cutaway, moves with ceremonious distinction ; stops three paces from desk*). I have the honour, Herr Reich Chancellor.

HITLER (*has risen*) : I have the honour, Your Excellency. (*Comes with agile movements to the front of the desk, shakes hands ; both remain standing.*) Your Excellency wishes to see me urgently. I'm happy to be able to receive you.

THE AMBASSADOR : I thank you for your invitation,

Herr Reich Chancellor. I regret to have to disturb you at this somewhat unusual hour.

HITLER : I trust the time's not inconveniently late for Your Excellency. (*Sits at small table ; gesture.*) Won't you sit down. ·

THE AMBASSADOR (*sits*) : Thanks. It's not too late, Herr Reich Chancellor. In any case—better late than never.

HITLER : The popular sayings are usually true. It was my experience when I lived among the people as a working man and (*emphasis*) as an out-of-work that the spiritual make-up of the worker and the peasant never lacked the bent to recognise basic truths and the ability to express the fundamental truths of a sound, natural, practical life concisely, in a popular and frequently humorous way. (*Emphasis.*) The people are the greatest philosophers, (*gesture*) the people as a whole, in the mass.

THE AMBASSADOR (*courteously nods agreement*).

HITLER (*as though brought to himself by the nod*) : But perhaps that's enough of mass psychology. I trust Your Excellency is well.

THE AMBASSADOR : Thanks, Herr Reich Chancellor, yes. The weather's fine.

HITLER : A particularly fine late summer. (*Significantly.*) Ideal for manœuvres. (*Emphasis.*) An old front line fighter like myself associates everything with military ideas. (*Objectively.*) I don't wish to encroach on Your Excellency's valuable time unduly.

THE AMBASSADOR : Your time's still more valuable, Herr Reich Chancellor. With your permission I will explain the object of this urgent visit. My Government has been viewing with deep anxiety the development of the international situation, and particularly German-

Polish relations, during the past forty-eight hours.   My Government, actuated by a love of peace, would like to examine whether it could usefully collaborate in relieving the tension and in the peaceful settlement of the questions that are undoubtedly waiting for a solution.

HITLER : No one desires peace more than I, Your Excellency.   The success and the lessons of the task of internal pacification accomplished by National Socialism have filled me with the conviction that every dispute can be settled without war, provided (*somewhat reproachfully*) that the desire for an understanding is not one-sided and that the aims of both parties or (*strong emphasis*) all the opposing parties are clear and their desire for peace is sincere.

THE AMBASSADOR : My Government entirely agrees with you in this matter.   But the finding of peaceful solutions requires time. . . .

HITLER (*somewhat rudely interrupting*): I've already proved many times that I possess an extraordinary amount of patience.   (*Menacingly.*)   But it's not unlimited.

THE AMBASSADOR (*continues, imperturbably*): . . . and a calm atmosphere.   One of the chief causes of my Government's anxiety is precisely the fact that it cannot see this calm atmosphere in the development of German-Polish relations.

HITLER (*involuntary outburst*): That isn't my fault. No one can expect a calm atmosphere when Germans are being massacred in a foreign country.   (*Controls himself.*)   Perhaps Your Excellency does not know about the official reports received concerning the atrocities committed against the German minority in Poland ?

THE AMBASSADOR : I do not know about any official reports, Herr Reich Chancellor.   All I have seen are the private despatches and articles appearing in the German Press. The tone of these articles, or shall we rather say the whole Press campaign, is so extremist in character that the question arises whether the true facts are consistent with the unmistakable tendency to incite the population with a view to certain action.

HITLER : No one's entitled to doubt that the German Press is telling the truth !

THE AMBASSADOR (*refusing to be drawn*) : Herr Reich Chancellor, you will probably remember quite clearly the Press campaign that preceded the annexation of Austria.

HITLER : Schuschnigg had let power slip from his grasp. He threw it away. He let loose the . . . (*gets stuck for a moment, then*) the mob ! There was German blood flowing in Austria before I made order there. That was what the German Press reported.

THE AMBASSADOR (*evades this, too*) : It's just a year ago that the other Press campaign began ; it dealt with the alleged anti-German persecution in the Sudetenland, in a similarly violent tone.

HITLER : It was not alleged anti-German persecution, Your Excellency. At that time the Czechs were torturing and killing the German minority.

THE AMBASSADOR (*imperturbably proceeding along his own track*) : Naturally, Herr Reich Chancellor, you also remember very well the Press campaign that was carried out at the beginning of the present year, before the Czech President's Berlin visit, the theme of the campaign being the same as before, with the same tendency, the same object and (*mild emphasis*) the same final result.

HITLER (*somewhat uncomfortably, yet menacingly*) : A united nation reacts to identical situations in the same way !

THE AMBASSADOR : That is precisely the circumstance which my Government views with so much concern. The German Press and, through it, German public opinion, is under a central direction in accordance with the axioms of National Socialist ideology. At the same time international relations do not evolve of their own accord and, similarly, international conflicts are also made.

HITLER : Everything in the world is made by men. The theory is not far removed from my view; but I reject the insinuation hidden behind it. (*Suddenly*.) Don't let's beat about the bush, Herr Ambassador, there isn't time. We're talking about the German-Polish dispute. Well—I must have Danzig, the Corridor and Eastern Silesia back. I must get back every square foot of German soil. I must get back every German soul. And if they're not returned I'll take them back. Naturally, therefore, I have to be prepared for action in every way. (*Menacingly*.) Well, I am prepared.

THE AMBASSADOR : Herr Reich Chancellor, you made a ten-year pact of friendship and non-aggression with Poland five years ago. You recognised and publicly declared that a people like the Poles need the sea and are therefore entitled to an outlet to the sea.

HITLER (*mild irony*) : Poland is a great country, but Germany's greater still. And if Germany's interests are in jeopardy I will know my task. My tasks are determined by the destiny of the German people, and the destiny of a people is not a dead thing, like a scrap of paper, it lives, develops, changes. I direct the destiny of the German people, therefore I'm responsible for it, Herr Ambassador.

THE AMBASSADOR : An historical task, an historical

responsibility, Herr Reich Chancellor. There's only one responsibility that's greater—responsibility for the destiny of humanity.

HITLER (*ignores this ; continuing*) : And if during the performance of my task the instruments of peace fail me I shall not hesitate for one moment to use the instrument of war. (*Hypnotically.*) Yet it's peace I want, and no one must doubt that I'm prepared to keep the peace.

THE AMBASSADOR : I'm convinced that Poland does not doubt it, either. That is why she on her part is ready to make any sacrifice for peace that will not involve injury to her vital interests, to her national dignity, to her sovereignty.

HITLER (*vehemently*) : What about Germany's vital interests ? And Germany's dignity and sovereignty ? A nation of thirty millions cannot oppose a nation of eighty millions !

THE AMBASSADOR : Historical justice does not dole out rights according to the size of populations.

HITLER (*loses his bearing ; shouting*) : I'm not going to adapt myself to historical justice—I make historical justice ! I will not allow Germany to be humiliated, I will not allow my people to be deprived of its right to live, to be shut off from its natural lebensraum. (*Excitedly.*) The whole world knows that if my present demands are met I shall have no further territorial claims in Europe !

THE AMBASSADOR : Herr Reich Chancellor, after the annexation of Austria you declared that you had no further territorial claims in Europe and expressly assured Czechoslovakia of your disinterestedness in connection with her. After the annexation of the Sudetenland you declared that you had no further territorial claims in Europe.   After the annexation of the whole of Bohemia and Moravia you declared that you had no further territorial claims in Europe. (*Without emphasis, sudden change of tone.*)   Poland is nevertheless prepared to negotiate and prepared to come to any rational agreement.

HITLER (*suppressed rage, ironically*) : Prepared. . . . Kind of the Poles.

THE AMBASSADOR : If all your wishes are met by peaceful agreement, what guarantees can Poland (*emphasis*) and Europe have that the sacrifice has not been in vain ?

HITLER (*screaming*) : My pledged word ! Who says that's not enough ! If I say that *this* is my last territorial claim in Europe, if I say that after the satisfaction of my claim (*contemptuous gesture*) all the nations, large and small, can live as they like, it's nothing to me . . . if I say that I will raise those who are my friends and let those who're not my enemies get on according to their way and their abilities, who says that's not enough ? Who says my word's not enough ?

THE AMBASSADOR (*cautiously*) : My Government has always regarded the pledged word, the contract, the undertaking as sacred.

HITLER : That sentence. . . . (*Brief pause.*)   There's a reproach hidden behind your words, your accents, Herr Ambassador.   Or is it a threat ?   Your Government has made certain undertakings to Poland. (*Savagely.*)   Do you think that means that you can incite the Poles against me ?

THE AMBASSADOR : My Government has proved more than once that they're prepared to make sacrifices themselves, as well as induce our friends to do so in the interests of peace.   But my Government holds that peace without honour is unthinkable. And the sort of peace that begins by depriving a nation of its honour, then of its means of life and in the end probably of its separate existence, its independence and free-dom——

HITLER (*interrupting*): Are you talking about Versailles, Herr Ambassador?

THE AMBASSADOR: Herr Reich Chancellor, my Government has proved that they are prepared to consider the peaceful and equitable revision of every mistaken and outdated provision. That is precisely why they cannot look on inactively while further mistaken arrangements are being developed, possibly by the application of force.

HITLER (*stares at him savagely for a moment*): It depends what you regard as mistaken. (*Sudden change of tone.*) Who's resorting to force? Who wants trouble? Herr Ambassador, let's be candid. I don't want to hurt anyone who's not hurting me. But this sort of passivity is not worthy of Germany, nor of your nation, indefinitely. We're both great peoples, great nations, great Powers. If we face each other as enemies—that's the downfall of Europe. If we stand side by side—that's the beginning of new, tremendous progress for the world. (*Wide gesture.*) Let's complement each other. Don't let's be petty. Czechoslovakia, Poland . . . bah! Don't let's scribble frontiers on maps, or mess about with miles, villages, a hundred or a thousand inhabitants. There's no doubt as to the ratio of power, there's a natural balance, all we have to do is to recognise the situation and have the will for collaboration. (*Low, firm.*) The Continent belongs to me, the world to you. (*Gloomily.*) I'm not greedy.

THE AMBASSADOR: My Government cannot haggle

over the destiny of other nations, Herr Reich Chancellor.
My Government cannot consider any other policy than
to recognise and, if necessary, defend the right of every
free people to its own free and independent life.   My
Government is well aware that European civilisation
will reach an unprecedented crisis if our two nations
come into conflict with each other.   But this crisis will
befall Europe just the same and will even extend to the
whole world, if free and independent nations had to
submit to force, if under external pressure they had to
abandon that for which they have lived : their form of
life, convictions, philosophy, economic possbilities, in
a word, their national existence. (*Brief silence.*) Herr
Reich Chancellor, my Government will undertake any
sacrifice and suffering, if necessary, but they will not
tolerate that Europe should become a continent of slaves.

HITLER (*ironically, his voice rising*) : It needn't *become*
that—it is that already.   It's only the blind who cannot
see, only the imbecile who cannot recognise that the
whole world is one horde of slaves.   There are only
two master nations—mine and yours.   The whole
world is waiting for a master to lead it, keep it in check,
punish it when necessary, in a word, make it happy.
That's what they all want, black and white alike : their
daily bread and a flogging at the right time.   Our two
nations are destined to rule. (*Beside himself.*) Herr
Ambassador, I'm not in the habit of begging for things.
And I don't offer anything twice.   Europe's mine, the
world's yours !

THE AMBASSADOR : My nation would not be worthy
of freedom and honour if it did not respect the freedom
and honour of other nations.   My Government wants
peace, peace with every nation and for every nation.
But not at *this* price.

146

HITLER (*suddenly, coldly*) : Then your Government's not going to support my just claims ?

THE AMBASSADOR : My Government will recognise every just claim to the utmost limit of justice and reason.

HITLER (*is silent for a moment, with compressed lips, then*) : So your Government will support Poland if she resists my will ?

THE AMBASSADOR : My Government will carry out in accordance with the laws of honour and humanity all their obligations freely undertaken. But I emphasise once more, Herr Reich Chancellor : Poland of her own accord, as well as upon the advice of my Government, is prepared to make *any* sacrifice if she can thereby really ensure peace.

HITLER (*darkly*) : It's not the first time I've extended the hand of friendship towards your nation, and not the first time it has been refused. (*Menacingly.*) But perhaps I've offered it for the last time and you've refused it for the last time.

THE AMBASSADOR : My Government has received and will always continue to receive with gratitude and understanding all your well-intentioned approaches.

HITLER (*darkly*) : Your Government, Herr Ambassador, thinks that there are nations who are in need of tutelage and there are nations who are entitled to be the guardians. (*In a stifled voice.*) The German people is not going to have any governesses. (*Outburst.*) I've the greatest army in the world and if it comes to a break . . . my Germany is not going to lose a war !

THE AMBASSADOR : My Government is convinced that it's possible to win peace . . . for humanity . . . without war.

HITLER : If I give way ! If I humiliate myself ! (*Brief pause.*) You, Herr Ambassador, spoke about historical responsibility just now. (*Bellowing.*) Now I'm going to talk about responsibility! And I disclaim all responsibility!

THE AMBASSADOR: The responsibility is ultimately fixed by history itself, Herr Reich Chancellor.

HITLER (*in a strangled voice*): So Your Excellency's Government is determined on war. (*Outburst.*) You don't know what modern war means! Whole cities will be wiped out by aerial bombardment, tens of thousands killed, hundreds of thousands made homeless. There'll be no safe and peaceful hinterland in modern war. War to-day is not a conflict between armies but the life-and-death struggle of the whole nation, of the whole people. In modern war the stake is the survival or complete annihilation of the adversaries. Modern war is hell, Herr Ambassador!

THE AMBASSADOR: No doubt it is, Herr Reich Chancellor. And no doubt it is hell for all the belligerents.

HITLER (*suddenly rises; coldly, formally*): I thank Your Excellency for your kind visit.

THE AMBASSADOR (*rises*): I thank you for receiving me, Herr Reich Chancellor.

> *They shake hands. The* AMBASSADOR *retires with formal bearing.* HITLER *walks behind desk, stares before him for a moment, then his hand crashes on a bell-push. The shrill sound of the bell is heard both off and in the room.*

THE ADJUTANT (*instantaneously appears*).
HITLER: Send them in.
THE ADJUTANT (*vanishes*).

> *After a few seconds the National Socialist General Staff crowd in, headed by* GOEBBELS, GOERING *and*

HESS. *There are a number of generals among them. The door is closed. The group lines up facing* HITLER.

HITLER (*for a short while faces them mutely, with his head lowered, then he jerks his head erect, fixes the line with his eyes ; low*) : I've decided. We march.

> *The stage suddenly darkens ; a black curtain drops in front of the scene, but the stage curtain remains up ; pitch darkness.*

THE RADIO (*in the darkness, at an abnormal pitch*) : The position of the German minority has become intolerable, the hour of mortal danger has struck. In the frontier districts the Poles are killing our German blood brothers by the hundred, subjecting German children to inhuman torture, raping and torturing to death German women. The Fuehrer will not tolerate this deadly insult to Germany ! (*The screaming voice becomes inarticulate, then intelligible again.*) The Fuehrer fixed fair and acceptable terms for Poland. But Poland did not even send her representatives when she was invited to discuss the Fuehrer's terms. Behind the Polish arrogance there are the machinations and incitements of the Western Democracies, Britain's ambition for world power, France's traditional hatred of Germany. The pluto-democracies are out to destroy National Socialist Germany. (*The voice changes to inarticulate bellowing, then becomes intelligible again.*) During the night Polish troops invaded German territory. After the intolerable provocations we now have open threats and actual invasion. Poland has attacked Germany ! The Fuehrer disclaims the historical responsibility for the outbreak of war, but he will not tolerate that the soil of National Socialist Germany should be desecrated by the tread of barbarians. The Fuehrer has

ordered the repulse of the attackers and an irresistible
advance for the protection of our German blood
brothers and the restoration of order.   The Fuehrer has
given orders. . . . The Fuehrer has given orders. . . .
(*The voice becomes inarticulate, merges into another kind of
noise ; the darkness is filled with the tramp of marching feet,
the deep bark of distant guns, the rumble of tanks, the roar of
armoured cars and motor-cycles, the rat-tat of machine-guns,
the throb of cruising warplanes, the screech and crash of bombs.*)

CURTAIN.

SCENE IV

Early autumn, 1940. HITLER'S *study in Obersalzberg. At
back, vast window looking on the mountains. In front
of it large desk littered with maps. Right, globe of huge
dimensions. Sliding door in right wall. Plain desk
with several low-backed chairs downstage left, beyond it,
on the wall, a life-size portrait of* HITLER *in black
frame. The entire interior is strictly utilitarian.*

*Dusk. The Alpine glow and the reflection of the
clear deep blue sky penetrate through the window. It
gets gradually darker, until there is complete darkness
outside.*

HITLER *is alone in the room.*

At the rise of the curtain

HITLER (*is standing in front of the large window, with his
back to the audience, gazing out at the mountains. After a
moment he turns round, comes forward, walks to desk on left,
picks up a paper from it, looks at it, puts it back, turns to
face his own portrait, stares at it for a second or two, suddenly
turns away, crosses to large desk at back, bends over it to look
at maps, straightens up ; he stands still for a moment, then
he walks to the globe, stares at it ; slowly his right hand rises,
he slowly rotates the globe, continent after continent passes
before his eyes ; low*) : The whole of it.   Completely.
(*Gives the globe an impatient swing ; it makes a few quick
turns, then stops ; he turns away, comes farther forward ;
low.*) I've succeeded so far. Seven years. Quick work.
How long will the rest take ? (*Walks to large desk, leans
against it.*) What's the cost so far. A lot. Nothing.
I'd have given a hundred times more. I've got plenty.
(*Straightens, crosses to smaller desk, stops, stares at portrait,*

*his arm involuntarily rises to the Nazi salute, but drops
before the gesture is completed ; speaking to the portrait, low.*)
What's going to happen next ? (*Suddenly turns and backs
away, again turns to face the portrait, stares at it ; low.*)
I'm going to destroy Britain. I'll have London bombed
into rubble. Churchill goes to Dachau. (*Low, with
strangled rage.*) They didn't want my friendship. (*Low
croaking, with reminiscence in his tone.*) They can't humiliate me ! Even God can't humiliate me. (*Rattle in his
throat.*) I'll smash the British Empire. The British'll
be my most wretched slaves—slaves of my slaves.
London's superfluous.· The British people are superfluous. (*Sudden throb of planes through window ; he listens
with anxious expression, takes a few uncertain steps, as
though about to run away, then he controls himself, walks to
window ; the throb becomes louder, fades, becomes louder.*)
Planes. (*As though reassuring himself.*) My own. The
night patrol. They're guarding me. (*Turns, faces audience from behind large desk, leans on it ; sudden changed tone,
low, plaintive.*) I'm tired. . . . (*Touches forehead.*) Here
. . . sometimes there's pressure. (*Low.*) It ought to've
happened differently. They ought to've surrendered
peacefully. They ought to've given in to me without
war, all of them. They can't do anything against me.
Why didn't they realise it ? Why did they force me
to—— (*Breaks off ; throb of planes off becomes stronger ;
the glow in the mountains is snuffed out, it is dark ; plaintively.*) Why didn't they let me accomplish my task in
peace. Someone must be master of the world—well,
it's me. Why did they interfere with me. (*Walks to
picture, gazes at it.*) I'm not a bad man—why do they
hate me ? (*Bellowing.*) I'm not a bad man ! (*It is now
pitch-dark outside ; the room is illuminated by a bluish-green
radiance from an invisible source ; suddenly.*) Who's that ?

Is there anyone here? (*Swings round, walks to door, returns ; natural, somewhat reproachful tone, as though speaking to someone in the middle of the room.*) What do you want again? Didn't I tell you I was not seeing anyone this evening. Let me be. Can't I have an hour's rest. Besides, why go over it again. (*Raises hand.*) It was your fault, Roehm. Why did you conspire against me? You didn't understand, either, you, my only friend, that I'm master, that you could only be my subordinate. It would've been all right for you—it's a great thing to be second in command to me. But you were disloyal to me, just like the other rogues around me, only your disloyalty was different—it was dangerous. The others cheat me, mislead me, they're thieves, big and little—I know and I don't mind. But you wanted my life. (*Plaintively.*) And if things had turned out differently you'd have done to me, in the end, what I did to you. (*Bellowing.*) Stop reproaching me! I won't have it! Your worst fault was that you didn't understand (*grinding his teeth*) that I'm not a bad man. (*Tearfully.*) I love little children. (*Stares vacantly in front of him for a moment ; vehemently.*) Leave me alone, man. You bore me. (*Sudden change of tone, as though continuing another conversation.*) Sorry, Schleicher, it was entirely your fault. You might've understood ; you didn't have to turn against me. (*Jerks his head up.*) I didn't tell them to kill Frau Schleicher as well. You're responsible for that, too. (*Minatory.*) A soldier shouldn't mix in politics. You could have built up the Reichswehr under my direction. (*Gesture.*) You wanted something else ; you got it ; I couldn't help it. (*Change of tone ; he turns in another direction.*) Can't you understand, Schuschnigg—my parents are buried in Austria. (*Plaintively.*) Was it right that there should be a frontier

153

between me and them that I couldn't cross? (*Low.*)
I once struck my mother. (*Changed tone.*) We're Germans, Schuschnigg, both of us. (*Gives a start.*) I can't
help it if you failed to understand me. I must unite all
Germans in a single empire if I'm to accomplish my
highest aim. Germany is power, the greatest nation in
the world, and I'm master of the world. (*Plaintively.*)
Was it right to interfere with me and hinder me in
that? Can't anyone understand me in peace? You're
responsible for what's happened. (*Low, persuasive.*) You
might've been converted to me, Schuschnigg. (*Changed
tone, turning in another direction.*) You ought not to have
resisted me, Pastor Niemoeller. No doubt your intentions for Germany are not bad, but mine are better.
No one must turn against me. I'm not a cruel man,
but I must prevail. (*Loud, indignant.*) It wasn't I who
invented the upright stone coffin in Dachau. It was
Himmler who had it made. I don't say that anyone
should be tortured to death. It's their fault, because
they failed to understand me and resisted me. (*Tragically.*) No one understands me. I'm alone. (*Low,
snarling.*) The Jews—they deserved what they got.
They deserve everything. They laughed at me. They
wanted world power for themselves. (*Bellowing.*) Who's
to be master of the world—they or I? I'm going to
be good to everybody (*cunningly*) who understands me
and believes in me. They must deserve my goodwill.
(*Changed tone.*) I didn't say that they should bomb and
machine-gun the refugees on the roads of Flanders and
France. It's part of the modern warfare. (*Explanatory
gesture.*) A new technique. My own technique. To
break the morale from the inside, prevent the manœuvres
of the opposing army by driving columns of fleeing
civilians across their path. Those who cannot under-

stand that this is a humane and considerate method
because it speeds up victory—let them perish. (*Low.*)
Why don't they love me? I live on herbs, I've no
woman, I've no understanding for wealth. They fête
me, yes, but they ought to love me. How will they
think of me when I am no more? Am I going to die?
(*Low.*) I am, perhaps sooner than I expect . . . perhaps
before I've completed my task. Who is going to carry
on? Who is going to finish it? How will they do it?
They'll spoil everything. I know (*contemptuously*) my
collaborators. I know who's going to follow me.
(*Febrile tone.*) Knaves, weaklings, fools. (*Heavily.*)
Everything's going to collapse, to dissolve into nothing-
ness. What'll be left after me? Masses of useless stone
and hatred . . . what a wilderness. (*Suddenly.*) I'd
like to sleep. But they keep coming and disturbing
me, they won't let me sleep. (*Walks to smaller desk,
sits in a chair, lets arms drop.*) I'd like to sleep, I can't
sleep . . . for the last five years, ten years. They
come and chatter, they exhaust me, then they leave me
by myself. I don't like to be alone, I can't sleep, anyhow. I lie down, I sit, I stare. . . . Then the others
come, the others, and they look at me silently. (*Jumps
up.*) It's no use, I tell you! Conscience was invented
by the Jews to paralyse the will. I killed mine! I have
no conscience! I'm not afraid of anybody! (*Low.*)
I'm not to blame for anything. It was I who was
right. They ought to have banned the Party, jailed
two dozen leaders and hanged a few, then the movement would've been at an end; but they didn't do it.
It was I who was right. (*Comes forward.*) If they'd
joined hands against me in Parliament and the country,
what could I have done? To-day I'd be an exile somewhere in the world. But they didn't do it. It was I

who was right. The people didn't want me, but they allowed themselves to be played into my hands; I was right. I used force, they shrunk back and surrendered to me; I was right. They were afraid of me at a time when they could still have crushed me. They cringed before me, served me, submitted to anything; I was right. (*His voice gradually rises.*) I knew what I had to do and did it; no one resisted me either within the country or abroad. And whoever does resist gets crushed in the end. (*Walks to globe agitatedly, stares at it; low.*) Europe. (*Gives it a slight turn.*) Africa. Asia. Australia. America. The North Pole, the South Pole, the islands, the seas. (*Brief silence.*) I'm creating a new world, a new humanity (*turns to face the audience*), God alone can create! I am God. (*Gives a nervous twitch.*) Who am I doing it all for? (*Stands rigid for a moment, gives a start, hastens to door, listens, turns the key soundlessly, hurries back to smaller desk, faces portrait; low.*) Satan! (*Listens.*) Do you hear me? I want you! I'm summoning you! You promised to come when I call you. (*Penetratingly.*) I'm calling you now. I must speak with you. (*Stands facing portrait with extended arm—a summoning but also a saluting gesture.*)

> The portrait in the black frame suddenly comes to life, its features have changed to those of Satan. A mild red glow merges with the bluish-green radiance at his appearance.

SATAN : What is it, Adolf? What do you want of me?

HITLER (*slightly breathless*) : You're here! Excellent!

SATAN (*steps out of frame and near the smaller desk, facing* HITLER ; *stretching himself*) : What a rotten lift—narrow and cold. It's cold here, too. (*Angry.*) Surely, there's no shortage of fuel at your house ! Fancy, the difference between Hell and Obersalzberg is one hundred thousand and thirty degrees centigrade. (*Dispirited.*) Having made a direct link between our residences you might've made it more comfortable. You pulled down and re-built whole cities, made *autobahns*, a thousand other roads and ten thousand other superfluous and osten-tatious structures, wasting labour, stone, marble, iron, concrete on senseless and rather inartistic things, and you had to skimp this one lift-shaft ?

HITLER (*humbly*) : Forgive me, Master, I was think-ing only of myself when I had it built, in case I had to flee one day . . . to the safest place and quickly. When you're escaping a mousehole or a mole's tunnel's enough.

SATAN (*impatient*) : Stop these almanac wisecracks. We're not at a party meeting.

HITLER (*plaintive*) : I never troubled you—this is the first time I've summoned you, yet you're irritable and impatient. Did I deserve this ?

SATAN : Don't let's be over-sensitive. What do you want ?

HITLER (*silent for a moment, then, naturally, but cautiously*) : I thought it was time I reported to you.

SATAN : Well, I'm not exactly without my sources of information, you know—and I'm not interested in details. I really expected your report when you could have simply said : I've done it. As far as I know that's not yet the case—or is it ?

HITLER (*cautious, evasive*) : I appreciate it very much that you're not petty and pedantic. I myself (*sweeping gesture*) am a man of grand designs. The details are for the experts and executive organs. But perhaps it'd do no harm for me to give you an outline of what I've done so far. (*Charmingly sulky.*) You really can't take it amiss if I even brag a little about my work. (*Casually.*) Besides, Master, there are one or two things we must discuss. (*Points at chair with comic, clumsy man-of-the-world gesture.*) Won't you sit down.

SATAN (*sits in large armchair at desk*).

HITLER (*looks at him queerly for a moment, then suddenly sits in the smaller chair opposite*): I'll give you a summary of events, with your permission. (*Narrative tone.*) When I returned from our last meeting (*gesture*) down there I set to work immediately. I must confess it was easier than I expected. They had prepared the way for me at Versailles very efficiently. Germany was prostrate and lay on the ground scarcely breathing, but she was not quite dead. (*Contemptuous gesture.*) The victorious democracies did their work very cleverly—they didn't kill Germany, as they could've done, but neither did they cure her, so that she should be in order for several centuries. They left that to me. (*Ironically.*) I'm grateful to the victors. (*Casually.*) I'm digressing a bit, but I'd like to observe straight away that I made a *different* sort of armistice with the good French and that the peace I'm going to dictate will also be different. (*Gesture.*) It'll be a complete job. (*Official tone.*) To get back to events in chronological order—after Versailles there was complete chaos, the situation was intolerable, hopeless. We started the Party. . . . I got your favourite number as a member—number seven. (*Low, dangerous.*) I have started a world revolution, the eternal evolution of mankind's new era. (*Narrative tone.*) Our success was immediate. The discontented, the despoiled, the hungry looked to us for their salvation. My crowds grew from day to day. (*Low.*) The women helped me. It was among them that I became a prophet. Enthusiasts and desperados flocked into my camp. The young, the generation of to-morrow, swarmed round me. (*Casually.*) I'd one attempted putsch that went awry—it was not bad as publicity, particularly as they locked me up for it for a time. In prison I wrote . . . (*cough*) with Hess . . . my Bible. It proved to be good business. Soon after, they let me out. (*Emphasis.*) They didn't execute me, though they could've done so. Nor did I catch pneumonia in jail as did so many of our prisoners later. There was not even a gun fired near me, not even by accident, as happened later, when I came to power, in the German prisons frequently enough. (*Importantly.*) The greater part of the proletarian masses came to my support and so did the capitalists. Clever, wasn't it? Both thought I was working for them. (*Self-satisfaction.*) Well, I did work . . . for myself. . . . Apart from a few sideslips everything went as I wanted it. There were many demonstrations, a lot of riots, a large number of Fehme murders. They worshipped me and feared me . . . (*flattering*) as you predicted. I could long have destroyed all public order and crushed my enemies, but I thought it wiser to enter into the game of Parliamentarianism—so we held election after election. We became the largest party in the Reichstag, though we didn't have an absolute majority. But I had patience. There came the crises, then the last grave crisis : I graciously accepted power from the hands of that senile old man. (*Low laugh.*) Everything was done constitutionally. Then we fired the Reichstag—a fine trick, wasn't it? Then I stopped the joke of constitutionalism. I was able to set about the internal

reorganisation of the country, according to my own
conception. I dissolved all parties and other organisations, sent my political opponents partly to break
stones, partly for a long rest cure, lest they should
strain themselves. A good many perished in the concentration camps. For example, it's no small matter
to stand at attention from morning till night in light
clothes in thirty degrees of frost. That was quite a new
thing, though by no means the only innovation in this
line. My experts really achieved a great deal in realising
my conceptions. (*Confidentially*.) I really think Himmler
could act as consultant even down below. He has
invented better tricks than even the best executioners
of Torquemada. (*Objectively*.) I made a bonfire of all
the books that the whole world valued, but I didn't like.
The Jews . . . (*gloating*) the Jews are a fine thing—
you can always do something with them. And the
success I've had in this field ! Outlawing them, depriving them of one right after another, sundry persecutions,
tortures, humiliations. It started a new migration and,
for example, I heard of a world-famous old Jewish phil-
osopher who became a cobbler in Bolivia—amusing,
what ? (*Dreamily*.) The Jews won't forget me for a
long time. (*Changed tone*.) The *Gleichschaltung* was a
good job, the National Socialist revaluation of all
values even better. I twisted the sense of words inside
out, confused established concepts. If you'll allow me,
I'll give you a few examples. Twenty armed SA men
attack and beat to death a single Jew—that's courage.
To execute without a trial—that's justice. To lie—
that's honesty. To steal other people's property—
that's the new right. To murder—A German duty.
And the new concepts I've created ! (*Proudly*.) *Lebensraum* ! Reich Chamber of Culture ! Blood and Soil !

Racial conscience! Blitzkrieg! Do you like them? They're in accordance with your spirit—they don't mean much, but they're fine instruments of destruction. I stopped cultural progress, transformed the old morality; (*vehemently*) it was I who put an end to the medieval era, it was I who introduced the real New Era. (*Gesture.*) But to go on. I began to rearm and at the same time I began to work abroad. The whole of Germany became a single armaments works, so to speak, a single barracks, a single drill square—and my agents reached every corner of the globe. (*Sly laugh.*) Just imagine, Master, a lot of countries refused to admit the refugees, but when my (*emphasis*) tourists and commercial travellers and visiting students and surveyors appeared the barriers were raised for them and offices, homes, institutions, human hearts all opened up to receive them. They organised torchlight processions and serenades for my agents and spies. Splendid, what? (*Proudly.*) My people got in everywhere—into the works, the big concerns, the cultural key points, even the administrations. I organised a *gau* in every country. I waved a finger here, and there was strike over there, sabotage at another place, unrest everywhere. Discontent spread, my teachings spread. (*Changed tone.*) I left the League of Nations, and although I still went on making international agreements they were only taken seriously and observed by the other contracting party. (*Giggles.*) The Polish Pact, for example—what a trick! (*Gesture towards left.*) It frightened the West, (*gesture towards right*), it frightened the East, and it (*gesture in front of him*) lulled the Poles to sleep. Then I settled accounts with my internal enemies. (*Stops, turns his head painfully in his collar, gives a cough, looks to the side; reassured.*) Then came the Saar. I won, of course. I had worked on the territory before the plebiscite. Then there was the abrogation of the disarmament pact. (*Mocking tone.*) Result abroad : general blue funkery, while here we were rearming, in the air, on land, at sea, to the utmost limit. (*Sweeping gesture.*) I did a complete job. Then came the re-occupation of the Rhineland ; then the open, official reorganisation of the Wehrmacht. (*Soap-box tone.*) I restored Germany's sovereignty. At this point I had to reassure the world a bit. I said I had no quarrel with it, all this was an internal affair, almost a private affair—no concern of foreign countries ; I wanted to live at peace with everybody. They believed me. The idiots. They could've crushed me, but they preferred to put their heads under my jackboot. (*Dreamily.*) At home there was order, perfect order. (*Sweeping gesture.*) I was destroying and made it seem as if I was building. A magnificent avenue across a city, aslant of it, in place of a thousand buildings. New German legal codes. New German literature, art, music ! Strength through Joy ! Schools for leaders and a new German education in general. I changed the masses into a herd of driven cattle while in my Ordensburgs I raised a new generation of leaders. How splendid is the youth I have created. I have killed their intellect and feeling, released in them the primeval instincts. How glorious that new youth ! Strong, determined, daring, unrestrained, Lords of Creation—beasts. (*Casually.*) Infant mortality became greater than at any time before me. (*Satisfied gesture.*) Church, family, private life—I settled all that properly. (*Gloomily.*) Then came Austria. There'd been a little cat-and-mouse play before, but now I annexed it. (*Incidentally.*) Suicides have reached an unprecedented peak. . . . The foreigners got frightened again, started to ring the alarm, but when I said this is all I want and no more they believed it again. The next was the Sudetenland, Munich (*laugh*). " Peace with honour in our time." . . . Then I took what was left of Czechoslovakia and started the war of nerves. Memel—a wink. Goebbels was really good. I myself was quietly preparing both at home and abroad. Not without success. (*Is beginning to be carried away by the sound of his own voice.*) I had a little rehearsal arranged in Spain ; it was a new thing to machine-gun civilians from aeroplanes. It was a brilliant success. We also tried out our new bombs and dive bombing. In a word, it was not entirely without practical experience and (*self-satisfied*) in accordance with my own well-thought-out plans that we went for Poland at dawn on the first of September. When it was over—sooner than I expected—we hibernated a little, so to speak, only just long enough to embody a few lessons in my tanks, sub-marines, bombs and planes. (*Maliciously.*) Over there there was real hibernation. (*Mysteriously.*) Well, then there was my secret weapon. Do you know what it was ? (*Triumphantly.*) *My saying it.* The effect was the same as if I'd really had one. Joking apart, however, I really do have a secret weapon. (*Sweeping gesture.*) My spirit. It's seeped into everything—into society, politics, institutions, the family—and every-where in the world. It gnawed and ground itself into things, preparing the soil for me. Then there's my shadow. It loomed over every country. They were afraid of me. They came to beg for my friendship, my favour—and they betrayed each other and what they used to regard as their ideals. They didn't ally them-selves against me in time until it was too late . . . then there came the psychological moment for me. . . .

The pigmies! They whiningly emphasised their neu-
trality and hoped, each of them, that I'd spare them,
only them. (*Naturally, almost naively.*) Why should I?
Why? (*Romantically.*) All quiet in the West . . . so
the first winter passed. (*Cold narrative.*) Then came
Denmark, Norway; then Belgium, Holland, Luxem-
bourg. Everything had been well prepared, from the
inside. It took only a few days. Next there followed
the Battle of France. There, too, everything was
worked out and worked up in advance. (*Rising voice.*)
I even had time for internal affairs—theirs. Himmler
was always immediately on the spot with the Gestapo.
(*Meaningly.*) He made order. (*Dreamily.*) New concentration camps . . . hunts for people in the woods.
. . . (*Objective tone.*) First, they perished by the hundred thousand on the roads, from my bombs, machine-
guns and tanks. Just imagine, Master, the spectacle—
a seventy-ton tank wading into a crowd of ragged,
footsore women and children trying to escape. The
new German æsthetics. I saw to it that the men in the
opposing armies—the fathers, husbands, brothers,
fiancés—should learn about it—(*laugh*) of course, in the
sense that it had all been done by the British. Then I
swept the civilian masses from one country into another.
Over a million Polish workers into South Germany
—for forced labour. A hundred thousand Dutch-
men into Austria—for forced labour. Out of their
homes! Out of their native countries! (*Emphasis.*)
Exchange of populations—that's another new invention of mine. Good, isn't it? (*Gesture.*) In any case,
there are no frontiers any more. There's only Germany.
(*Objectively.*) What food and raw materials the foreigners
had I took away. We needed them—but we needed one
thing more: that they shouldn't have them. (*Gloomy.*)

Dunkirk . . . something went wrong there. I imagined that differently. (*Angry.*) But I've started the air
war against Britain. (*Grows morose.*) The British are
tough and cunning. (*Plaintive.*) They camouflage their
military objectives as homes, churches, hospitals,
museums, their aerodromes as parks and squares, their
barracks as schools, their armament factories as
cinemas and theatres. But I detected the ruse ! They
resisted fiercely. (*Bellowing.*) They've hit back !
(*Beside himself.*) I'll invade and destroy Britain ! I'll
reduce London to ashes ! England will be my *Gau* of
Desolation !

SATAN : That'll be a good thing. But tell me, how
did your ally Mussolini turn out ?

HITLER (*angry contempt*) : You might've spared me
such an ally. He's bad even for publicity when I have
to meet him on the Brenner. Instead of him helping
me, I've got to get him out of the mess. He was
clumsy even when he stabbed the defeated France in
the back. (*Menacing.*) He's dreaming of a Roman
Empire, the half-wit. Side by side the German World
Empire (*ironical emphasis*) an " Imperium Romanum " !
(*Menacing.*) I'll give him an Empire. Let me finish
with the rest—I'll see to the Italians then. (*Beside himself again.*) The world's going to be German and
National Socialist ! I'll sweep the British Empire off
the face of the earth. I've got Europe one way or
another. Whether I've got to crush the nations first,
one after another, or whether they surrender to me of
their own accord comes to the same thing in the end.
Africa's next. I'll conquer it. Egypt, the Suez Canal,
Sudan—I'll march down east and west simultaneously
to the Cape. My armies are awaited by peoples made
ripe for revolt against their present rulers, and they'll

hail me as their liberator. One jump towards the East—
Asia. India will rise and submit to me. (*Ironically*.) I'll
pacify the Indians all right. I'll also attend to my Bolshevik friends ; it won't be a hard job. (*Low*.) I'll
make the Russians realise that they can get only from me
what they really want. China I'll break with the aid of
my other ally, Japan—but the power will belong to me
there as well ; as you might imagine I shan't let that
yellow mob have it. Why, a handful of rice—that'll
be their reward. Then it'll be the turn of Australia and
the South Sea Islands. All I have to do is to send my
fleet ; its very appearance will be enough. And if not,
so much the worse for those who resist. America is
encircled and isolated. I'll attack her in the North and
South at the same time. I've been unremittingly gnawing at her vitals for a long time. At the right moment
she'll fall at my feet, and if not I'll force her to her knees.
(*Snarling*.) I've got my enthusiasts and hirelings there
also, ready for action at their key-posts. I only have
to give a bark to make the dollar crash. (*Low*.) Gold
is ever a coward. The people credulous. All I have to
do is to promise prosperity ! They can't oppose me !
I'll have the continent surrounded by ten thousand
submarines—I'll simply let them stew in their own
juice until they come and beg for mercy, and if they
don't come I'll have two hundred thousand bombers
for them. When that's done I'll organise a few expedi-
tions to take possession of the Polar regions and any
unexplored continents. Then I'll inaugurate the New
Order in the whole world. (*Rising voice ; feverishly*.)
The New Order ! Do you know what that is ? A
colossal pyramid as big as the world—with me at its
peak, me the leader, the Law—below me the elect, the
sub-leaders, my Power—below them the Party and the

Gestapo, the Control and Executive—beside them the new German youth, the future, the Succession—below them again the German people, the master race, the keepers of order, the Overseers—and far below them all the other nations, the Slaves. My New Order! Two peoples : the Germans and the rest. Two classes : the possessors of rights and the servants of duty. Two ranks : the strong and the weak. Right will be the Right of Might. Justice will be the Prerogative of Strength. Morality will be the ethics of Brawn and Force. The spirit will be the Spirit of Instinct and Passion. The New Order. . . . I'll transform the face of the world, nature itself, the body and soul of man— and when this is done, then I'll be able to say : I've done it.

SATAN (*with satisfaction*) : It'll be a great job, no doubt. And when it's finished I'll take over.

HITLER (*as if he hadn't heard*) : The only army in the world will be mine. There's no other force, no other power but me. (*Rising voice.*) I'm master of the earth —I'm the first real master, greater than the Pharaohs, Nero, Attila, Jenghis Khan, Napoleon and the Kaiser rolled together. Men and things will serve me, the elements will obey my commands. I'm stronger than the floods and the earthquake, my power is greater than the power of gold and all the human passions, my influence greater than the instinct of self-preservation and the fear of death. I've saturated the earth as the plague saturates its victim, I've done a more complete job than the most devastating prairie fire. I raise a storm and it blots out the sun. The lives of men and the destinies of nations depend on me. The world feels and thinks according to my commands, for my will is law. They worship me more than God and fear me more than you.

SATAN (*surprised*): It seems as if I'd heard this before . . . as if I'd said it myself. . . .

HITLER (*still louder*): What does it matter who said it first? The facts speak for themselves. A little longer and everything will be fulfilled. (*Sudden.*) Master! Let's clear up the relationship between us. The agreement I made with you is bad!

SATAN (*taken aback*): What do you mean—bad?

HITLER (*violently*): It's bad—bad for me. And my reward's too small. I perform the task with which you've entrusted me, then I can go to Hell to roast the damned. I didn't think the matter over properly at the time.

SATAN: But you made a contract with me!

HITLER (*naïvely*): What of it? Since in the meanwhile the contract has proved to be bad it must be revised.

SATAN: You sold me your soul.

HITLER: Well, you've already got it. You extracted it from my body with your own hand. Don't you remember? To me the operation was useful.

SATAN: You gave me your word!

HITLER: Under the pressure of the political facts I hereby withdraw it.

SATAN: You're breaking your word? Revolting against me? I made you! You've been my instrument!

HITLER (*laugh*): That's what they thought, too. Hugenberg the simpleton, the heavy industries and all my other so-called supporters. They thought they could use me and when I've done what they want they can throw me aside. Are you making the same mistake? They didn't know that I was more than human; but you . . . you haven't forgotten that I'm but little less than yourself. . . .

SATAN : I'll crush you——

HITLER (*interrupting*) : That's what they wanted to do. They didn't do it because they didn't dare and couldn't. . . . (*Low, menacing.*) For instance, General Schleicher . . .

SATAN (*suddenly, very embarrassed*) : But . . . I don't understand. . . . What is it you want ? Aren't we fighting for the same cause ? You got the commission from me, I supported you and . . . (*Amazed.*) I wouldn't have believed *this*.

HITLER : Don't let's be over-sensitive. (*Low, menacing.*) Our aim is the same, don't let's spoil things by turning against each other, Master. But . . . (*menacing*) if necessary, I'm game. You can't do anything against me, you can't undo anything, whereas I——

SATAN (*gives visible start*).

HITLER : ——I can. And if that's the only way, I will not recoil from it. You can't get the Earth if I don't want you to have it. (*Menacing.*) My army's better than yours. My soldiers can bear the terrestrial climate, yours cannot. My weapons are mightier, more modern, more lethal than yours, and . . . I may's well tell you . . . I've got a secret weapon . . . a simple weapon, it resembles the hilt of an old-fashioned sword . . . (*low*) . . . it's the shape of a cross. . . .

SATAN (*suddenly raises his hand in front of his face*) : Adolf !

HITLER : And if I give my policy a new twist and issue a new slogan with the New Order—With Hitler against Satan.

SATAN (*claps his hand to his forehead*) : But really——

HITLER (*continuing, menacingly*): But don't you think that I'll only have Man to support me. I'll have others. (*Meaningly.*) Others, many of them, who're discontented and ready to revolt, who're only waiting for a sign from me, waiting for my armies . . . waiting (*points downwards*) for me to come and liberate them. (*Gesture.*) Down there. . . .

SATAN: Down in Hell?

HITLER (*naturally*): Why not in Hell? (*Penetratingly.*) My teachings have taken root there as well. My agents have occupied the key positions there as well. I'll be candid: I've already selected my Protectors, my Governors, my Hell-Gauleiters . . . indeed, I've already thought of a new dynasty . . . it's someone from your own tribe, because it's my custom and because a wise foreign policy demands it; the name of the pretender is . . . (*Bends forward, his lips forming a name.*) Rrr . . . (*Suddenly.*) No, I'm not going to tell you—yet.

SATAN (*scream*): Runty!

HITLER: I didn't tell you. (*Sudden, incisive.*) But don't let's pursue this. It's something else I want, if you agree. Now that you know my strength and power you must realise that it wouldn't be good for you to resist me and that if it comes to a conflict between us it might well be fatal for the cause of world evil. I want to remain friendly with you. I appreciate the help you've given me and I don't wish to be ungrateful. But I want to be on terms of equality and you must admit that I'm a partner, not a mere tool—though only a modest partner. I'll deliver the soul of Man to you, but the Earth . . . (*Jumps up.*) What use would it be to you? (*Hurries to globe, gives it a spin.*) What is the Earth . . . as compared with the whole? (*Returns and faces* SATAN.)   You must be wise and generous.   I acquired the Earth, so I keep it.   I don't even ask for immortality—my successors and disciples will continue the affair for a million years . . . a thousand years. . . . (*Suggestively.*) You're entitled to more. Leave this trifle, reach out for something bigger.

SATAN : What's all this ?   What do you want ? You can't cheat me.

HITLER : Don't oppose me, I beg of you, don't turn against me and don't force me to turn against you. (*Bends over desk.*)   I don't want to hurt you if you yield to my will.   I want to be kind to you if you will only understand me. (*Imploring.*) You must understand me. . . . You must understand me.   There's plenty to share and who should share (*sweeping gesture*) the *whole* if not we two ?   And I'm a modest man.   I want the Earth—all the rest is yours.

SATAN (*backs away, with chair, half-rising in it*) : What . . . I don't understand . . . what do you want ? . . .

HITLER (*at the peak of agitation*) : They are too old and exhausted up there !   They manage things badly. How long do they want to stay in power ?   We've had enough of them !   There is chaos in the Universe ! You should establish a New Order !   Go up to them, bang your fist on the table, say that the Original Contract is bad, so it binds you no longer, and if they refuse to accede to your demands, then you will act. Wrest the power from them.   You have the strength and the brains and if, in addition, you have the courage, you'll win !   Your followers are the master race of the Universe.   Up till now, you've been a poor devil— make yourself lord and master of the Universe.   The suns and solar systems, the Milky Way and all the stars will be your servants.   You've got the will and the ability. (*Encouragingly*.) If you like you can have my latest stratosphere dive bombers and spheric parachute squadrons !

SATAN (*upsets chair behind him, backing away*) : You——

HITLER (*raving*) : Leave the Earth to me—occupy THE WHOLE ! We two together . . . I down here . . . you up there and everywhere . . . for evermore. (*Waves arm.*) Sieg Heil !

SATAN : Away from me . . . Satan ! (*Jumps into the frame on the wall and vanishes.*)

HITLER (*stands with extended arm facing his portrait*).

Sudden blackout. There is a sound as of a siren.

SCENE V

*The stage is in darkness. The whining sound of the previous
    scene is heard fading away. A pale blue radiance illu-
    minates a small part of the stage, downstage right; in
    it appears*

SATAN (*panting, beside himself*): Lord! Where art
thou, O Lord! Canst thou hear me, O Lord! (*In a
panic.*) Lord, O Lord!

> *Upstage left, high up, a golden light rises, from it
> comes*

THE VOICE: What do you want, Satan?

SATAN (*falls on his knees*): Help, O Lord! I'm in
peril. . . . The experiment has failed. . . .

THE VOICE: What have you done, Satan?

SATAN: I lost control—to the creature of my creation. The thing that has happened is beyond my
powers. I undertook something and have failed—but
at least I want to save my honour. *This* is not what I
wanted, O Lord.

THE VOICE: What do you desire me to do?

SATAN: Forgive me, O Lord, and repair what I
have sinned against Thee and against Man through my
creature. Turn thine eyes upon the Earth once more
—accept Man back into thy mercy—and deliver him
from evil. (*Touches the ground with his forehead; the pale
blue radiance is snuffed out.*)

THE CHOIR (*off stage*): For thine is the kingdom, the
power, and the glory, for ever and ever, Amen.

THE VOICE: Michael! Gabriel! Raphael!

MICHAEL ⎫ (*appear   simultaneously   in   a   fresh   blue
GABRIEL ⎬ radiance   on   the   right*):   What   are   thy
RAPHAEL ⎭ commands, O Lord?

THE VOICE : Repair and cause to be repaired what the Evil One has sinned through his creature against me and against Man. Return to Man the Earth, to the Earth return Life, to Life render Beauty, Loving-kindness and Justice. Give back its meaning to human existence according to my law. Give back to humanity its Faith and Honour. Make order down below—My eternal Order. That is my will.

MICHAEL ⎫
GABRIEL ⎬ Thy will be done, now and for ever-
RAPHAEL ⎭ more, Amen.

> *They turn to face audience, raise their trumpets to their lips ; there is a mighty blast ; there is a distant roar in the darkness. Mixed choir and orchestra offstage strikes up softly, then grows louder as the scene develops, intoning triumphant Anthem of Freedom.*

MICHAEL : Righteousness ! I summon thee.

A VOICE (*from a rising spot of light*) : At thy command.

GABRIEL : Wisdom ! I summon thee !

ANOTHER VOICE (*from ditto*) : At thy command.

RAPHAEL : Beauty ! I summon thee !

THIRD VOICE (*from a different spot of light, like all the following voices*) : At thy command.

MICHAEL : Honour !

GABRIEL : Humanity !

RAPHAEL : Strength !

VOICES : At thy command.

MICHAEL : Courage and Loyalty ! I summon ye !

GABRIEL : Loving-kindness !

RAPHAEL : Self-sacrifice !

VOICES : At thy command.

MICHAEL : All the hosts of Virtue—Mind, Knowledge, Zeal ! I summon ye !

GABRIEL : All the hosts of Virtue—Spirit, Faith, Purity ! I summon ye !

RAPHAEL : All the hosts of Virtue—Determination, Perseverance ! I summon ye !

VOICES : At thy command.

MICHAEL : Spirits of the brave and honest, arise !

GABRIEL : Spirits of the tortured and humiliated, spirits of the deceived and betrayed, arise !

RAPHAEL : Lovers of the Light ! Watchers of the Night ! Ye who stand for Truth and Justice and Freedom ! Arise !

VOICES : At thy command.

MICHAEL : Raise up your hearts against Evil.

GABRIEL : Raise up your spirits against Destruction.

RAPHAEL : Raise up your fists against the Corruptor.

VOICES (*from all directions, in thunderous chorus*) : We will !

MICHAEL : Raise the banner of Justice.

GABRIEL : Add strength to Truth.

RAPHAEL : Support the struggle of the Brave.

VOICES (*as above*) : We will !

MICHAEL : Nations of the Earth, arise—the Lord commandeth !

GABRIEL : Ye who are oppressed, behold, redemption is at hand !

RAPHAEL : Ye who are enchanted, awake !

MICHAEL : Furnaces and forges, pour forth your weapons.

GABRIEL : Blessed be the weapons that fight against Evil.

RAPHAEL : Ye men, grasp your swords ! Ye women, stand firm !

VOICES (*from all directions*) : We're ready !

MICHAEL : Forward against the scourge of humanity.

GABRIEL : Forward against him who has enthroned grief and hate upon earth.

RAPHAEL : Forward to Salvation and Peace.

VOICES (*from all directions, filling the entire stage*) : Salvation and Peace !   Salvation and Peace !

> *A flourish of trumpets rising crescendo ; a heavy rumble from all directions ; the spots of light that have come up one after another now fill the stage with a brilliant glow.*

CURTAIN.

THE END

(*London, October–November*, 1940.)